ON HIGHER GROUND

ALSO BY WILLIAM D. GAIRDNER

The Trouble with Canada

The War Against the Family

Constitutional Crack-up

ON HIGHER GROUND
Reclaiming a Civil Society

WILLIAM D. GAIRDNER

Published in 1996 by
Stoddart Publishing Co. Limited
34 Lesmill Road
Toronto, Canada
M3B 2T6
Tel. (416) 445-3333
Fax (416) 445-5967

Stoddart Books are available for bulk purchase for sales
promotions, premiums, fundraising, and seminars. For details,
contact the Special Sales Department at the above address.

Canadian Cataloguing in Publication Data

Gairdner, William D. (William Douglas), 1940–
On higher ground: reclaiming a civil society
ISBN 0-7737-2939-9

1. Canada – Social conditions – 1971–   .*   2. Canada – moral conditions.
3. Canada – Politics and government – 1993–   .*
4. Social values – Canada.   I. Title.
HN103.5.G35 1996   306'.0971   C95-933295-2

Cover Design: the boy 100 & Tannice Goddard
Computer Graphics: Mary Bowness
Text Design: Tannice Goddard

Printed and bound in Canada

For my Father
and Mother

CONTENTS

PREFACE

This book was born on a happy day in spring 1994 through the union of two unforeseen circumstances.

First, we discovered that the farm to which our family had moved needed a lot of unexpected attention, at about the time that our three youngest children experienced a growth spurt which produced in them a diabolical appetite for more school, sports, and social activities. So in addition to a heavier than normal year keeping our small business together, my wife and I found ourselves busier than ever, driving all over the map, grateful for our few quiet moments together, very late at night. All this led me to wonder how in the world I was ever going to find the concentrated time and energy for another book.

"You're not, just now," came the answer from a little voice inside. "So why don't you write one on the installment plan instead?" In other words, instead of worrying about time to build a house, just start making the bricks. After enough bricks are in place, the house will take shape. This idea caught my fancy as much as it reduced my anxiety. I would fit the next book into my life, instead of my life into the book.

Shortly thereafter, through a nice bit of serendipity, the second thing happened. An unexpected telephone call came from Murdoch Davis, editor of the *Edmonton Journal*. He said he was concerned — it bothered him — that some people accused his newspaper of being "left wing," whereas he was one editor who truly believed in a broad spectrum of considered opinion. He had read some of my work, thought it would help serve as a balance (I was going to say, a corrective), and wanted to know if I would consider writing for the *Journal*.

I immediately liked his sincerity, and his commitment to broad and serious journalistic dialogue. I was also intrigued that a Southam-owned newspaper would ask a writer known for his deeply conservative, traditionalist views to do a column. This was like offering me a Trojan Horse. I would have a chance to do intellectual and moral battle from inside the walls (though I'm quite sure Murdoch would debate energetically who was on which side of those walls!).

I told him that I was flattered by the offer but had never knowingly written anything that I knew with 100 percent certainty would meet the fate of all newspapers the very next day — the trash can or the fireplace. Somehow the idea of concentrated disposable expression was not terribly appealing. We finished by agreeing that I would try doing a few columns to see if both of us liked the result. Fair enough.

Straightaway, I called my publisher to see if he had an interest in a book of serious short pieces more or less anchored in current events, in which I would attempt to draw out the logic and moral of national issues in a very short space.

The answer was an energetic encouragement to proceed. That did it for me. My weekly effort would now be preserved in a more durable form. This seemed quite fitting, because my complaint about all so-called social democracies is that relinquishing personal and community responsibilities to governments has the dangerous effect of softening the mind and the will; of turning what ought to be enduring moral debates and standards into disposable opinions, values, or perspectives, as the state leads us towards one bankrupt utopia or another. ("Perspectives" happens to be the name of the page of his newspaper for which Murdoch wanted me to write, and the irony of a man who believes there are enduring truths, writing for a page of perspectives, will only be lost on the most committed pluralist.)

At any rate, whenever this great softening of the national mind and will occurs, the people can be roused, indeed, and vigorously, but only to demand their rights, or to reject their duties — the latter increasingly seen as a bothersome obstacle to their rights.

Yet perhaps the greatest duty of a free people is ongoing profound and conscious deliberation of the core legal, political, and moral issues of their day. A positive, energizing, community-building result of this is always desirable, rarely achieved. The very best practical result, therefore, is that these matters — the very sort considered in this book — at least continue to turn in the lively fires of the public mind and, if possible, cause ongoing discomfort. For if not, the mind sleeps, the ground shifts beneath our feet, and we awaken to find ourselves in a different country.

So when struggling to find a title for this book, I explained to my wife, Jean, that what I wanted most was to elevate the debate, to somehow pull readers up to a . . . to a . . . and she said the words: "higher ground."

And the book was born. I am confident that at the heart of each piece there is a well-developed, well-defended argument that stands up in debate. In almost every piece I believe I have been able to show that once we agree to leave behind our personal or factional or — most commonly — emotional self-interest, there is indeed a higher ground from which these issues ought to be considered, for the greater good. That's why my hope for the reader is that this book will give great pleasure, some insight, and perhaps a little discomfort.

* * *

Sincere thanks are due to close friends and family who offered commentary on many of these pieces, or had the patience and grace to put up with me as I worked my arguments on them. Thanks are also due to Murdoch Davis for his adventurous invitation, and the Trojan Horse, and to the many feisty letter-writers in Edmonton who sometimes filled half a newspaper page with their reactions.

Not last, by any means, are the thanks due to Don Bastian and Angel Guerra of Stoddart Publishing, who separately and together always give great encouragement, and who worked closely with me on this book.

WILLIAM D. GAIRDNER

I

It's a Question of Vision

Where there is no vision . . .
the people perish.
But where there is sham vision,
they perish even faster.

— *IRVING BABBITT*
DEMOCRACY AND LEADERSHIP, *1924*

A TYRANNY
OF INDIVIDUALS

THE ANCIENTS WERE RIGHT. The more things change, the more they stay the same. History is not progressive. It is cyclical. Greed, ambition, duplicity, self-interest, and above all the lust for power — these are the things that drive history — so what's new?

The democratic twist on power was to put it in the hands of elected representatives of high repute: properly educated and respected persons with high ideals. But recent Angus Reid Polls — can you believe it? — say our politicians get a measly 4 percent rating for "respect" from the public. *Four!* Why, even a hose to empty a septic tank does better than that. Journalists and lawyers weren't much better, at 15 percent and 11 percent, respectively.

At least when respected sages spoke of the eternal rhythm

of things and the need to be good, everyone agreed that there were, in fact, such things as goodness, truth, honesty, and integrity. When they asked themselves what purpose life had, they came to the general conclusion that it must be more than mere pleasure. It was the pursuit of those higher things, for oneself, and for society. It was possible to agree on what is good.

A prominent French anthropologist, Louis Dumont, divides all civilizations accordingly. A "holistic" society — the kind everyone claims to want to live in; you know, a real, natural community — is unified by an ideology of hierarchical values. There is a shared notion of good, better, best, and bad. Ye olde praise and stigma flow accordingly, unifying all in the same moral bond. Sure, that's the right word. True freedom is the freedom to bind yourself, not to values (a gooey notion, like the word "perspectives"), but to principles and norms.

What he terms an "individualistic" society is the opposite. At the core of its ideology is "equality," the idea of freedom for all from oppressive authority. Originally, such folks just meant freedom from governmental or monarchical authority; from thumb screws and the rack. But eventually, the torture toys ended up in Madame Tussaud's wax museum, and the equal freedom campaign had to go on a search-and-destroy mission for ever-diminishing authority targets. Even ordinary praise and stigma would have to go, in the name of moral neutrality. Everyone would finally be diverse, pluralistic, and free from all moral judgement. That is, free from each other. You see the point. More of this kind of freedom means less community.

All societies must have individuals, of course, but the

distinction here is that holistic ones begin from a different premise. They recognize the individual, but not as the sole source of norms. Rather, moral and social norms come from something higher than the individual — never from government, but from the moral demands of a spontaneous society conceived as something more and better than the mere sum of its individuals.

Dumont argues that modern collectivist movements (fascism, communism, the welfare state) were, and are, in fact, not progressive at all. They are frantic forms of political reaction to lost community in a world that created its own spiritual void. They are an effort to impose an official holistic community from the top on societies that can no longer produce it naturally from the bottom.

The fatal paradox of our so-called "liberal democracies" is that we can't produce community because our political ideology has made a point of neutralizing the whole idea of norms on which community is based. That's why at the extreme of imposed democratic equality you get not "liberty, equality, fraternity," but secret police, the Berlin Wall, the Gulag. It's because the second term of the slogan betrays the first, that the third can only be gotten by force.

So liberal democracy is fast losing the legitimacy it had before corroding itself. A glaring schism has resulted, formerly suppressed by Cold War tensions but now so visible in public distaste for (and sometimes tragic shooting of) elites and opinion-manipulators of all kinds. It's visible, too, in the troublesome formation of private militias — a kind of alternative community poised against government. And in all democracies, as in France recently, we see demands for referendum instruments to satisfy muted electorates who can't get what they want through their own representatives. Democracy's active self-contradictions are at work.

Consider just a few key features of liberalism, and what has happened to them. Limited government? At one government employee for every 5.5 citizens, we don't have a "limited" government. We have more per-capita government than most countries in the history of the world, and a public debt to prove it. Equality? Entrenched in our highest legal document is a mandate requiring us to impose differential law, social programs, and rights on specified groups and regions — we have a kind of affirmative inequality. Free Parliament and Rule of Law? Unelected judges routinely take pleasure in disqualifying the people's duly made laws, and by legal legerdemain finding fanciful unspecified rights in our Charter. And so on. Those reading the entrails of liberal democracy will be mightily occupied for some time to come.

THE PAY-EQUITY FEEDING FRENZY

WE KEEP GETTING THE message that Canadian women can't make it on their own. So government will help them.

"Equal pay is a right," trumpeted Treasury Board President Arthur Eggleton over a recent Ontario settlement that took sixteen years to resolve. Public servants will be paid an extra $74 million — in lump sums of $58,000 to some!

Let me see . . . Here we have government employees, using government consultants, to mount huge claims against government institutions. It's a fiscal feeding frenzy the hapless taxpayer is powerless to stop. Current public-debt problems may back-burner this issue for a while. But the flawed thinking is here to stay.

Most of it is the work of a small army of white, middle-class radical feminists claiming gender discrimination to lobby for wages they haven't been able to command on their own merits in a free market. They lead the march to an unfree society.

In a recent television debate, I argued that feminists have been trying to substitute a coercive political order for our free economic order. It's like demanding that an ounce of lead and an ounce of gold command the same price simply because they weigh the same.

With great excitement, my opponent, an Ontario Women's Directorate lawyer, declared, "Yes, that's it — as long as they weigh the same, they should have the same value!" Medieval authorities repudiated the market in the same way, demanding a "just price" and a "just wage" by law be paid to all. Economic stagnation was the result.

The foundation of the "discrimination" charge used to justify programs like pay equity is the so-called wage gap. And indeed, there is a wage gap between the earnings of men and women. In fact, there are large wage gaps between all sorts of social groups: the young and the old, the educated and the uneducated, the experienced and the inexperienced, the hard-working and the lazy, the married and the unmarried, and so on.

Almost all of the women's wage gap is due to marital status. We know this because never-married women in Canada and the U.S. make exactly the same wages as never-married men. But when women marry, most quit, or scale down their work, to nurture their children. Conversely, when men marry, they aggressively seek more pay. Averaging married men and women indeed produces a wage gap, and always will, but it's dishonest to use this as evidence of discrimination.

The offshoot, so-called employment-equity programs, introduce an evil of their own. They force employers to hire "under-represented" women and visible minorities. And lots of men are lining up for unearned cash using the same arguments.

But if it's all right to force employers to hire certain under-represented minorities, doesn't it follow that in the interests of "balance" they should release, or refuse to hire, those from over-represented minorities? (Zap the National Basketball Association.)

I especially enjoy watching my liberal Jewish friends squirm when we debate this one. Jews are 1 percent of the Canadian population, but are vastly "over-represented" in many business fields like finance and property development, and in all the intellectual and professional fields. Good for them. They have a strong work and family ethic. But let's follow the perverse logic of affirmative action.

The last time I looked, Statistics Canada prepared a survey (catalogue 93-154, 1986) giving a long list of the average incomes of ethnic groups in Canada. Here is just a sample of the findings, top to bottom: Jewish, $40,093; Japanese, $30,750; Scottish, $29,393; Swedish, $29,018; English, $26,968; Polish, $26,754; Chinese, $24,073; Greek, $21,972; Caribbean, $21,493.

Now, are we going to argue that Jews, a minority whose ancestors came here poor and who have suffered vile discrimination throughout history, but who now outshine everyone by huge margins, are discriminating against the rest of us? Can we not sensibly argue that there is a bona fide "Gentile gap"? A "Polish gap"? A "Greek gap"? If not, then we have to argue that discrimination has made Jews high earners, and therefore ought to make women high earners.

Indeed, cannot those of us making less than workers from other ethnic groups apply to the Pay Equity Commission for lump-sum payments? And if not, why not? About ten million of us eagerly await our handsome cheques. Very eagerly.

In a riotous story, "Pastry Cook Pay Angers 800 Nurses" (*Toronto Star*, May 18, 1990), the full idiocy of these situations was revealed. After much precision and deliberation, the official job-handicappers of the state decided that a female nurse's job was equivalent to that of a male pastry chef. Well, the outrage! The scandal! The "unfairness"! Florence Nightingale — a pastry chef?

Pay equity was invented (a carefully chosen word) to make pay more "fair" for women who had voluntarily accepted their wages (remember, men in low-paying jobs are not allowed to apply for relief). But once the fairness judgement was rendered for nurses, these same women went on strike with placards, demanding "Fair Pay Equity"!

The biggest pay-off for this plunder has been from claims against government itself. But now it's creeping into the private sector. It seems never to have occurred to these women that any sensible employer will try to hire the best work for the least wage, just as any shopper will try to buy the best food for the least cost. And if hundreds of women line up for low-paying jobs, they will get low pay.

Ah me . . . I suppose that we will soon see droves of women who want even more money for nothing, demanding "Fair, Fair Pay Equity." But the employers will all have left town.

CON ARTISTS

CANADA IS A FASCINATING country. However, lately I am more frightened than fascinated.

Not long ago, on CBC Radio's *Arts Report*, I heard — oh, the sorrow! — a funereal male voice moaning over a tear-moistened script. He informed the nation that Toronto's ten-acre Harbourfront project, which holds 4,000 events and attracts 3,000,000 people every year, would soon close due to a 30 percent cut in its federal grant. Almost $9 million of Harbourfront's $17-million annual budget comes from Ottawa.

Correction. I just spoke "Canadian." It actually comes from millions of distant taxpayers who will never see Harbourfront, travels through Ottawa (where it is reduced by a sizeable commission), and flows on to grant-seeking artists and their ilk in Toronto, who for some unexplained reason cannot interest the public in paying them voluntarily. Therefore children's art, jugglers, ballet, modern dance, an authors' love-in, baseball games, poetry readings to other poets, all, all, we are told mournfully, will be gone forever.

Forgive the cynicism, but I smell special pleading. I smell the employees of a massively government-subsidized broadcaster weighing in with considerable muscle to slug it out on government-monopoly airwaves, with government ministers who are accused of cheapness (because twenty years too late they have reluctantly learned that subsidizing art contributes to our national debt).

This "arts" scenario is repeated daily by thousands of funded groups that regularly threaten to rally in their own cause. Too bad. Because Canada has some super artists in every field. But very few make it on their own. Most of them are snorting at the public trough. So their success can rightly be called artificial, because when government aid disappears, their art disappears. They are arts parasites.

Alarmed Canadian author John Metcalf bemoaned this halfway through the last decade, when he wrote that "the big commercial publishing houses are subsidized. The smaller literary presses are subsidized. The still smaller regional presses are subsidized. The writers are subsidized. The literary critics are subsidized. Translation is subsidized. Publicity is subsidized. Distribution is subsidized. More bizarre perhaps than anything else, the Writers Union of Canada is subsidized."

But the notion that government ought to subsidize art is a bad one that inevitably leads to poor art, half-empty theatres selling underpriced tickets, publishers warehousing books no one wants to buy, and hordes of deluded struggling artists who soon learn to tailor their artistic programs to please the granting agency.

To a great extent, the whole notion of public arts is the intellectually tattered brainchild of the world's statists, who still harbour deep anti-capitalist sentiments. Free markets are based on the exchange of inferior art for money only, goes this purist thinking. Millions of happy people who see schlock like *Phantom of the Opera*? Why, they need exposure to real art. Real artists make art not for money, but for the ethereal pleasures of art itself. Get market pressures out of the way, and then real artists can create freely, unpolluted by crass commercial limitations or cravings. So Act One, Scene One, is short: Hug government.

The paradox here, of course, is that in order to appeal for support, arts groups such as Harbourfront must convince us they are popular. Over and over we are told about the 3,000,000 visitors to Harbourfront.

So at once, my mind says, What's wrong with asking for ten or fifteen bucks apiece, the price of a movie with popcorn and a Coke? Somehow, that works out to $45 million at the top end which, less the budget of $17 million, would leave a profit of $28 million. Not bad for one season.

But instead of figuring this out, these spoiled artists start to cry. They would shut down, instead! They won't cut fat, fire incompetents, reduce expenditures, tailor production to meet demand, or just charge $5.50 per head admission to break even. No, they'll shut down the whole ten acres. Pout, pout. It's pathetic. I say let 'em stew in their own juice. Great art springs from great pain.

Meanwhile, check out people like Max Reimer, director of Huron County Playhouse in remote Grand Bend, Ontario. His Playhouse One theatre, stuck out in a country field, receives no government funding. "Not a nickel." The theatre has 614 seats, runs 129 shows per season at 94 percent capacity, and sold 67,000 tickets last year (at an average of $22 each). Grand Bend has only 600 residents, so the theatre must draw patrons from many miles away, 60 percent from London, a long 45-minute drive on a dark night.

Canada "is more than moose, mountains, and Mounties," says Max. "Top Canadian artists can be found in commercially successful productions all over the world. The good ones don't need government. C'mon up," he adds, "it's the field of dreams up here!" You bet.

Here's a final insight into this scary nation and its policy of subsidizing art: the separatist Parti Québécois, tenaciously dedicated to dismembering Canada, has published a manifesto entitled *Québec in a New World*. Inside the first page is a paragraph acknowledging, "with thanks," the financial support of the Canada Council.

GOVERNMENT JOCKS
AND JOCKETTES

"I LIKE THE HOCKEY STRIKE," said my neighbour. "It's the first time I've had the pleasure of booing so many millionaires!"

It was a laugh. But it got me thinking, and then grieving that all sport, pro and amateur, is no longer properly conceived. And that is sad, because sport, especially when done for its own sake, keeps us grounded.

Every child racing breathless through an autumn field, or carving an icy turn to snatch a speeding puck, or passing a ball to a friend who scores the impossible goal, has felt the thrilling capacity of sport to connect us. With each other. With the enduring truths and brute limits of power, courage, and ability. It's a great leveller, and teacher.

And sport has always been a kind of ideal for society, a

place where heroic effort and decent behaviour were possible in the context of the same rules for all. No political distinctions. Increasingly, however, sport is not an ideal for society but simply reflects its worst aspects.

Consider the pros: people who do sport not for itself, but for money. Not my cup of tea. Nevertheless, how do we react to the news that five years ago there were only five millionaires in NHL hockey, and now there are seventy-five? Well, despite the fact that no single citizen is exploited, or forced to buy a ticket, and televised sport is free, there have been howls of outrage.

Zowie. Here, from a bankrupt nation that in the mere space of thirty years has tried to control so much of political, economic, and social life that it is itself out of control — we get a knee-jerk control response to a growth industry that creates millionaires.

If pro athletes make "excessive" or "obscene" salaries, there is a call for "luxury taxes" on the successful teams, for "salary caps" on high earners, and for "minimum wages." We have an owners' union, a players' union, and now, Fans Inc., an Ottawa-based "union" for fans who figure they will soon have the financial clout to boycott sports.

Even sadder, however, is that amateur sport — sport for its own sake — has fallen to the corruptions of money, politics, and drugs. I say corruption, because you cannot do a thing for itself and also as a means to an end, such as a salary. The pay perverts the principle. Some years ago, the sport professor Bruce Kidd actually argued that all Canada's ranked "amateur" athletes should have a guaranteed minimum wage of $36,000 per year (again, from the taxpayer). Another professor argued seriously that taxpayers owe Canada's Olympic athletes "compensation for lost education."

Such talk about sport is just an expression of where the whole country has been headed for years: straight into an outwardly polite, government-nurtured holding tank for jostling, at-your-throat political groups seeking what are now ever-diminishing advantages from the public trough. Societies that go this route soon become control crazies. They see each other not as humans but as political integers. The concern becomes whom to envy, avoid, or avoid speaking about. Whom to fear.

Already, we walk gingerly with a frosted bubble over our heads. At first we see only shadows. Then, what could this be? Ah yes, I see now, it's aaaa . . . Black. There's another shadow. It's aaaa . . . White. And another. It's aaaa . . . Francophone. And here comes aaa . . . Turban. And this must be aaaa . . . Homosexual (oops, I mean a "Gay." Got to be careful, don'tcha know?). It's a recipe for alienation.

Canada is a country whose spontaneous cultural and community roots and values have been engineered almost out of existence by dreamlanders who happily substitute state policies and programs everywhere possible. High-level amateur sport has been taken over by the state.

The most destructive and subtle result is that the normal forms of community-based volunteer sporting activity, formerly so distinguished by proud independence from government, are diluted, then abandoned.

Alas, today's big-time amateur athletes are minions of the state, government-subsidized jocks and jockettes, many of whom get big advertising and prize money if they place.

Many literally bank on the secret use of drugs to win.

For my kids? No thanks.

Some of the honest "sport cripples" (because so undeveloped in other aspects of their lives), who hang on for money long past their useful prime, admit privately that without the commercialism, government dependency, and drugs, they couldn't succeed.

So to solve it all, I say let the market correct the problems of pro sport. They are openly beholden to money, but at least not to the state. As for amateur sport, except for the building of basic public facilities, we should get the state out of it entirely.

Then let's invent a sporting ideal kids can look up to, so communities can rely on their own local efforts to get the kids into those facilities and help them succeed. To be eligible, you have to have a job, or be in school. You can't be paid a penny. And drug use means banning for life.

We used to have something like that.

It was called the Olympic Games.

OUR NURTURING NIGHTMARE

Too OFTEN, A GUARANTEED way to ruin a good day is to read the morning paper. The execrable and morally lacerating descriptions of the Paul Bernardo trial simply reminded me how often I have had to junk the daily newspaper before the children see such bad taste and grotesquerie. Hiding a newspaper is surely cause to ask, What is happening to the world?

Ever since the decline of communism, the West has seemed in a state of accelerating moral uncertainty. It's as if, having spent so much effort telling citizens what liberal democracy is not, we have forgotten how to say what it is (which points out the value of a clearly defined enemy). It's not war but peace that is problematic, especially for wealthy nations whose citizens are unsure why they are alive.

Many are even asking the vertiginous question whether the core assumptions and values of liberalism and democracy might be mutually exclusive, for reasons no one can control. That is to say, is the idea of well-ordered freedom with majority rule by virtuous citizens a goner?

Think about it. Few dare to defend responsible freedom any longer (freedom is now licence, with no limits); majority rule has been trumped and circumvented (by interest groups, judges, and the Charter of Rights and Freedoms); and the classical virtues have been, uh, feminized.

Hold on. I say feminized, or womanized, because the Latin word "virtue" means "manly excellence," both in the plain sense of Man (we are humans, not animals), and in the sense of bold, disciplined virtues, shaping citizens for risk and heroism, against which the more feminine, nurturing virtues seek all-encompassing security. We need both in balance, but have lost just that.

What, after all, is Marxist socialism — any kind of socialism — if not an organization (at the extreme, a militarization) of society designed to appeal to our hunger for security — to what is most unheroic.

For better or worse, there have always been only two options: Leave people free to heroically take risks and organize their own security as individuals and families, with government restricted to minimal influence. Or deliberately assign the duty of eliminating all human risk to government itself, in exchange for government's total control of the people, their property, wealth, and work. You can't have it both ways. Alas, the second method necessarily entails the elimination of the manly virtues.

In classical times, these virtues were Prudence (doing the right thing at the right time); Courage (required to take risks); Temperance (self-limitation of the passions); and Justice (equality under the law for all). What is stirring about these virtues is that they have no meaning unless exercised by free men and women. But it was the clear conviction of the ancients that if citizens were not inculcated with these virtues (to which the later Christian era added Faith, Hope, and Charity — arguably more feminine virtues), democracy would soon deteriorate into soft, then hard, tyranny. For only a citizenry rich in the manly virtues could possibly stave off the equalizing tendencies of democracy that will always, if unchecked, eliminate shalls and shall-nots altogether, thereby destroying heroic notions of the good, thus raising the unworthy and lowering the worthy.

I've just received a mailing from the Council of Canadians imploring recipients to "Stand on Guard" for our "right" to health care, education, a pension, jobless pay, welfare, daycare, and . . . the CBC (!), things which I am told "bind us together as a nation." At least they could have said, "Give me security, or give me death!" But no such luck. No manly virtues here. Just gimmee, gimmee. Someone else owes me security, is the message.

Real dangers (such as hardened murderers, rapists, and burglars, patrons of our nanny criminal-justice system) walk the streets to strike again, while the media prattle on obliviously about false dangers such as "inequality," or "stigma," or "discrimination," or "inappropriate sexual touching." Have we become, as one writer put it, a nation of cowards? Any daily count of stories about things we now must fear tallies in the dozens. Is this the sign of a great people, this grovelling in what is petty, low, fearsome, and unequal?

We discover this same softening trend in the "Goddess" movement in the churches, in feminized university curricula, in politically fearful professors, and in the "Gaia" movement (where Earth Mother devours Sky Father) within environmentalist ranks. We sicken, too, of the silly, maleness-dissolving notion that our opposite genders are "socially constructed" and not an obvious, wonderful, and very exciting natural fact of normal biology around which all human life revolves; we especially sicken of the message that men and their manly values are bad.

Nonsense. All these are the sour grapes of politicized, security-drugged intellectuals who themselves feast on the impressive achievements of a risk-based male culture — only to criticize it. As the more honest (and feminist) Camille Paglia has put it, "If civilization had been left in female hands, we would still be living in grass huts." The dominance of the urge for security in men *and* women stifles achievement in individuals, and civilizations.

Better to have ordered freedom, natural biological differences, risk, and the manly virtues taught to children, I say, than the nurturing communist nightmare the world has left behind — or the softer version in our midst.

WHICH ONE IS THE WIFE?

Well, talk about a stunned silence. Our family was debating the Egan and Nesbit case which was before the Supreme Court of Canada. Two homosexual men who were reported to have lived "pretty much as a married couple" have claimed a right to spousal status and benefits.

Suddenly, in one of those defining moments that serves to focus a wandering argument, so that the reality warp that has everyone in its grip falls away before the clear light of day, my twelve-year-old son asked:

"Which one is the wife?"

That question will always ring in my ears because the obvious answer is — neither; for neither can ever be. And we can't argue "it's up to them," as in: you be the wife this week,

I will the next. For any society that abandons its ancient right to define, control, and most of all to discriminate over the terms of marriage, to the predilections of any two or more human beings that happen to share the rent, has abandoned marriage altogether.

Then it struck me that if we look beyond this particular case to the actual process at work in the court, we can see that Canada's Charter of Rights and Freedoms, in this and other cases, is being used as a battering ram to break down civil society. I wonder if the judges will see this process before it's too late?

For it seems there are only three ways we get controlled. Above us is the involuntary control of the state (as all too visible in the income tax). In the middle is the social control of millions of voluntary groups that comprise civil society (we voluntarily submit to the authority of marriage, the Boy Scouts, our corporation, and so on). And finally, at the bottom, there are millions of autonomous individuals exercising self-control (most of the time).

I contend that the egalitarian state has the effect (sometimes, the ambition) of breaking down the voluntary authority of civil society through its evangelical eagerness to equalize everyone under its own coercive influence. One way it does this (and in this respect, the courts become an arm of the state) is through Charter-style attacks on our ancient social right to discriminate between those who opt into social groups, and those who do not (who nevertheless are left alone with all their normal individual rights).

What we end up with is an unintentional ideological war between the state and society, the end consequence of which (the end purpose, in socialist states) is to weaken society and strengthen the state.

For all social groups rely on a kind of solemn rite of passage, the markers of which are sacrifice, subordination, commitment — and that nasty old thing called privilege.

Sacrifice refers to the requirement that individuals aspiring to join a social group must voluntarily agree to place the common will of the group above personal needs. The motto of common organizations like Rotary International, for example, is "Service Above Self."

Subordination refers to the requirement that all members must submit to the authority and discipline of the group. For infidelity, members get expelled, Boy Scouts get demoted, spouses get divorced.

Commitment is the process whereby the member who gets this far is asked formally to make a vow, or a public verbal or written commitment, to shared ideals. That's the bonding.

Privilege is the last stage, whereby society (sometimes backed by the law, as in family law) approves the bestowal of specific benefits and protections on each qualified member. That means money. Status. Approval.

All of civil society, we might say, is thus really a vast organism that hovers over the great undifferentiated mass of autonomous individuals, seeking not only to select, but to direct; to lure them into its own far more challenging and difficult social life. This is a process inherently preferential, and intentionally exclusionary, and the modern liberal project is to destroy it.

So we try in vain to imagine a world in which little boys — or girls — demand the right to wear Boy Scout uniforms without qualifying for them; where homosexuals demand the legal, tax, and even commercial advantages and privileges of married couples, without submitting to the difficult procreative sexual order of society (on which even their existence depends); where non-members claim the rights and benefits of membership in groups for which they have not qualified; where the rights of private and commercial property are brought down, and the natural propensity of all human beings to create meaningful positive social distinctions and privileges is driven underground.

When there is no meaningful society left, when it is sufficiently weakened, slack, and torpid, when there is intolerable crime in the streets and the schools, when drugs and disease mount their eager claims, when every window in every home is barred, when political and social cynicism reign supreme, there will be only one authority to consider: the all-controlling state, cultivating allegiance, even grateful admiration and obedience from its millions of autonomous and utterly dependent children, even as it crumbles.

We have brought this on ourselves in the name of rights and freedoms.

LET'S WRITE A CONTRACT WITH CANADA

WHAT A JOY TO SEE in the 1994 congressional elections and the '96 presidential campaign: a conservative U.S. Congress that vows to restore America to Americans; to rescue it, not from government, but from the state; from the largest, most entrenched class of interest groupies, social engineers, and tax-plunder specialists ever assembled in U.S. history.

For it is no mean distinction to say that while government seeks a framework for the maximal exercise of responsible individual liberty, and repudiates bureaucratic control of society (the democratic ideal), the state repudiates individual liberty in favour of forced equality through maximal bureaucratic control.

So this is no revolution. It's a counter-revolution.

It's the people reasserting their primordial values and standards against a whole generation of cynical egalitarians who imposed welfare-state regimentation on America, and created a dreadful civil war of values in the process.

Same for Canada. The 1960s saw hordes of leftists and credit-card hippies, one-worlders, draft-dodgers, feminazis, homosexual activists, and liberal dreamlanders of all stripes from all parties commandeer the instruments of power. I have said we now have one full-time government employee for every 5.5 Canadians. But if we discount children under 18, it's more than likely to be one for every three!

Americans have revolted against the revolution. Will Canadians do the same?

If their serious answers to simple questions are any guide (and if not, why do we ask?), the Republican "Contract with America" is not much different from what heartland Canadians say they want. But can't get . . . yet. That's because as in America, only some of our political parties are officially registered. The two most influential ones — the Court Party, and the Media Party — are not.

The Court Party is far more radical than the official parties, wielding power from the bench, from every law school in the nation, through legal journals, through funding, research, and "action" committees, and especially through the plethora of appointed "tribunals," "commissions," and "task forces" that constitute the unofficial government of Canada.

The power of the Media Party should not be underestimated, either. A few good ones notwithstanding, its membership largely comprises half-educated liberal scribblers who can't make it as writers or professors. But they can savagely ridicule or suppress any voice, distort the message of any book, and hysterically promote their preferred social agenda.

Despite this, it is exciting to think that just as the American people are finally in a position to take on their own president, the *New York Times*, and Harvard, Canadians may some day get the country they say they want.

The Contract with America calls for a balanced budget, a line-item veto, and capital-gains tax cuts. How refreshing. A revolt against legal plunder!

Just so, a decade ago (and repeated every year since) fully 84 percent of Canadians said, "Cut spending, don't raise taxes" (Gallup, March 16, 1986). But no dice. Instead, we have a per-capita total national debt (all three levels of government) almost twice as bad as America's, totalling over $1.3 trillion when unfunded liabilities are included.

Americans are also rebelling against crime. They vow to strengthen the death penalty, eliminate flimsy grounds for appeals, and stop pandering to criminals with mushy "rehabilitation" programs that mostly fool parole boards into early release.

What else do Canadians want? In May 1987, 61 percent told Gallup they wanted the death penalty reinstated, and 78 percent said, "The courts are too lenient with criminals" (Gallup, Jan. 19, 1987). What do they get? Pathetic bleatings from criminologists about how poor so-and-so, who brutally raped and murdered six children and seven old ladies, needs more sex therapy before his ten-year punishment expires.

And it's wonderful to see U.S. rebellion against the nefarious anti-family and anti-work ethic of modern democracies. Americans will limit welfare payments to two years, provide tax incentives for adoption in an effort to reduce America's wholesale abortion rate, give tax credits to encourage family care of children and the elderly, and end tax discrimination against marriage.

What do Canadians want? Eighty-four percent told Gallup that "welfare recipients should be made to work" (Nov. 30, 1989). An astounding 94 percent say they want "more emphasis on traditional family ties" (Feb. 4, 1989). A huge majority of 75 percent say flatly they "reject abortion on demand" (June 20, 1988). A distraught 76 percent say that "children's well-being is sacrificed because both parents have to work" (Globe/CBC poll, Nov. 1, 1991). A "whopping" 66 percent say "the best place for pre-school children is at home with their parents" and oppose "day care of any kind" (Decima, June 5, 1991). Fully 78 percent want to "increase family allowances to families in need" (Gallup, Oct. 24, 1988). And finally, an "overwhelming majority" want mandatory physical education in the public schools (Jan. 9, 1990), and an incredible 94 percent — almost everyone — want standardized evaluation in public schools (Gallup, 1985).

But we can't get any of it! So let's write a Contract with Canada — and throw the masters out.

DON'T NUKE
THE DUKE

CLEARLY, ROYALTY IS getting tired. Tired, at least, of the bleatings of such as Prince Charles and Princess Di, and the washing of their bed sheets in public. Millions of people the world over, their gossip meters pulsing frantically, could barely control those pesky images of Princess Di in the stables with her teacher, in a wild state of undressage, the straw flying everywhere. Or cheeky Prince Charles in his stocking feet, tripping lightly up the back stairs on his way to another difficult bout of infidelity with mistress Bowles.

In a bid to end it all, the Duke of Edinburgh sighed in a widely reprinted *Economist* editorial that "a republic is a perfectly reasonable alternative to a constitutional monarchy." By the term *republic* he meant a country free of monarchy and controlled by the people. *The Economist* agreed with the Duke. It is "against" the monarchy which, it solemnly declared, is "the antithesis of much of what we stand for: democracy, liberty, reward for achievement rather than inheritance."

Both statements are hard to swallow without a lot of chewing. For a republic is as much opposed to monarchy as could be imagined. It is even stranger to hear those words about democracy, liberty, and achievement. For Britain, Canada, and the U.S. are not true democracies. We seldom vote directly on issues. The first two are constitutional democracies under a weakened monarchy. And a graph of the past century would show that liberty and local control have retreated everywhere in the "free" world as monarchy has declined. Finally, to speak against inheritance is to speak against achievement itself, because people work hard and burn with pride mostly to help their families and offspring. A child's breakfast is a form of inheritance.

The whole fabric of our civilization is politically and socially inextricable from the monarchy, the fundamental purpose of which is plain. A European statesman explained it best when in reply to Theodore Roosevelt's question "What is the role of a Monarch?" he answered: "to protect nations from their governments." If we fail to see this, we see nothing.

For a monarchy can save democracy from what Austrian scholar Erik von Keuhnelt-Leddihn calls the "collective self-worship" that tends to blind us to truth, making democracy ripe for tyranny and eventually dictatorship. As he warns, any number of nations in history, starting with Greece itself — a democracy so alien to liberty it executed Socrates and exiled

Aristotle — have swung wildly from democracy to tyranny, to monarchy, and back again.

And the first modern expression of democracy — the French Revolution — included the beheading of King Louis XVI and ended with the massacre of a quarter-million innocent French citizens, by then described by their own government as the "internal enemy." Louis was put to death — democratically, in the name of the "General Will" of the people — by an extremely divided assembly that voted 387 to 334 in favour of beheading him. There was nothing general about it.

Part of the difficulty is that we have learned to equate democracy with liberty. We should not. Democracy is merely a technique for allocating power, and as such it has often been used to impose oppressive regulatory regimes (our own), or even elect despots. Hitler was an example. While no system is perfect, defenders of monarchy argue that the institution has much to recommend it as a method for containing just such excesses.

Unlike a democracy, which is based on divisive struggles for supremacy, and at every election becomes what von Keuhnelt-Leddihn calls "a solemn manifestation of division" (often producing "leaders" with only minority support — like Bill Clinton and Bob Rae), monarchy is above party rule. It is a unifying social as well as political principle for the whole nation, its people, and all political parties. Hence the phrase "Her Majesty's Loyal Opposition." After all, one cannot be loyal to Parliament itself, which is inherently fractious.

The primordial model for monarchy, of course, is the natural family, the basic hierarchical social unit of all civilizations, and (despite the musings of the United Nations) the farthest thing from a democracy. This model forms a triad for all Christian societies of Holy Family, royal family, secular family. And it is no happenstance that a coronation is a religious sacrament, for the most important forgotten truth about the divine right of kings is that monarchs were guided by publicly acknowledged duties to God and the natural law, and were severely limited by church and people to those duties. The reasoning here was that the people can always be fooled — but God can't.

Democracy, however, is the reverse. It derives authority not from publicly acknowledged transcendent ideals, but from shifting ideals and anonymous, secretly voting masses, on a purely numerical basis; on the *quantity* of decisions, not their *quality*. Thus we arrive at history's first mass cult of irresponsibility, in which elected officials can easily blame the people for their failed mandates. And so — von Keuhnelt-Leddihn again — for the first time in history we get "the immoral idea of making whole nations responsible for the misdeeds of their rulers, whether they had majority support, or not."

Hence the spectacle of self-righteous leaders plunging modern nations into bankruptcy and then receiving not a jail term, but gold-plated pensions.

Perhaps we should think twice before we nuke the Duke.

THE MYTHICAL MONEY MONSTER

IT CAN LEAP OVER tall buildings in a single bound. It can fly. It can swim. Soar. Roll. Gyrate. Fight. Shoot. Stampede. Why . . . it can do anything!

Is it a bird? Is it a plane? Is it Superman?

No way. It's . . . *the economy!*

This tireless mythical entity can be seen in any newspaper cavorting and snorting, or changing bodies and abilities, wreaking havoc with our dreams.

Its most common form is animal. The economy, the dollar, interest rates are described indiscriminately as a force outside ourselves with a life — and mind? — of their own. A charging horse, for example.

The rider is the people, eager to control and direct. There is talk of "reining back" interest rates, or else the dollar will be off on a "wild ride." Or the rate will "climb," or "fall." (Question: Why is the dollar said to "climb" up, but "fall" down? Couldn't it "climb down"?) Sometimes this frisky fellow can be caught "stampeding," or "rolling" suddenly, like my own horse, in the sand; or, in a moment of perkiness, it may actually "jump," for no reason.

Sometimes, just to elude economic soothsayers, the beast will transmogrify. Like Pegasus, the dull horse may suddenly sprout wings and "soar." Or, rakish and profit-hungry, may "dive," or perhaps just "hover" around the financial horizon searching for prey (our savings). Occasionally, like those theoretical visions so dear to evolutionists, the monster has both land and marine characteristics. After soaring, it may decide to "plunge," or even "plunge deeply," or "plunge suddenly," as if to surprise even itself, into an unspecified and bottomless pit, producing a horrible sense of vertigo.

One financial writer, fancying himself perched on some inviolate shore, announced that "the whale is back in the water" and warned that "the world" risked being "upended" if "the beast changes course and swims off in another direction." This gave a titanic sense of the entire globe, out there in the darkness of the universe, balancing precariously on the back of a flippant, entirely self-willed leviathan. A kind of inverted Moby Dick.

This is a worrisome image, and it contrasts poorly with the peaceful answer given the curious little boy who challenged his Hindu teacher's claim that the world rested on a turtle. On what does the turtle rest, then? And the reply was: Son, from there it's turtles all the way down.

In our most helpless moments, it seems, this mythical beast suddenly loses all distinctness. Wings and feathers are shed. All stamping and snorting cease and, as if in a horror film, our breakfast, our RRSPs, our children's education, everything, is abandoned to the unpredictable wiles of an amoeba-like organism, half animate, that simply "contracts" and "expands." Our worst fear is that it might grab us by the leg (a "debt trap"), or inexplicably start "gyrating." Or, disconcertingly, in a fit of ill humour, "fluctuate wildly," or "rebound" or — very personally — even "punish" us.

At such dire moments, either a crisis is "brewing" (sign of witchcraft) or "will deepen" (watch for peat bog, or quicksand) or we could have a Russian experience — "a meltdown" — or . . . (this is very bad) we could end up in "a financial black hole," sucked into nothingness by a force of gravity so strong nothing will ever escape.

By now, we can only wait and pray.

In better times, of course, there is a more defiant imagery of heroic combat and struggle, including missiles, jet planes, and guns. Companies and countries are said to "struggle to break even," which gives the effect of bursting chains in which, perversely, they have somehow wrapped themselves. We watch, helpless, as whole industries are "dealt a severe blow." Sometimes, a "mortal" one.

Governments are usually pictured "deficit fighting," or in a "deficit battle" (the business of spending more than is earned is presented as mysteriously beyond warrior control). Inexplicably, no one in government is ever fired, or jailed for this malfeasance. Rather, the earnest deficit fighter is cast as King Canute, slashing, on the people's behalf, at waves comprising disobedient dollars. This gives a deeper meaning to the name of the Canadian dollar, the "loonie."

In moments of true warrior optimism we are asked to accept heavy military and ballistic imagery. There are now deficit "targets." Warrior Finance Ministers and Corporate Captains will step gingerly through a "minefield" of voter (or shareholder) demands to "hit" the target. Or they may commence some action "triggered" by expectations that production will "take off," or "roar off the runway."

A favourite, too, is imagery of the Flood, with water, water everywhere. Mexico will be "sunk." Brazil "could get swamped." Canada is "awash" in debt. And the force? Well, it has become liquid, too. Capital "flows away," the "sluice gates" open to new investment. A most athletic and cocky investment counsellor describes how he just "hops on or off" the "tidal wave" of world currency flows.

Readers are forgiven for wondering what any of this has to do with our traditional vision of working hard, staying debt-free, and saving for the future.

II

ON CULTURE WARS

And so I hold it is not treason
To advance a simple reason
For the sorry lack of progress we decry.
It is this: instead of working
On himself, each man is shirking,
And trying to reform some other guy.

— ANONYMOUS, IN OHIO NEWSPAPER, 1920

PAROCHIALISM OF RACE
AND BLOOD

In THE FIRST QUARTER of this century, in a statement sandwiched between two bloody world wars, Julian Benda said that what defines our age is not any shared set of natural beliefs, but "the organization of political hatreds."

He saw coming our modern rejection of universal ideals, and the resulting embrace of raw political will, ethnic egoism, and (multi)cultural nationalism.

In this light, perhaps the most fatuous official pronouncement of the decade has come from Multiculturalism Minister Sheila Finestone, who declared that "there isn't any one Canadian identity. Canada has no national culture." First she says there is no unity, then proposes the illogical and perverse notion that plurality is unity.

But Canada has always been as diversely peopled as could be imagined and without a central focus of commanding ideals might easily have fragmented into cultural tribalism. Ethnic feuds over body type and blood. Struggles based on the dangerous notion that origin is destiny — rather like the Parti Québécois notion of the "peuple." (And remember how that tripped up Premier Jacques Parizeau!)

What has saved us to date has been the deep faith of our founders that British classical liberal ideals were better — far better — than competing ideals. And so it is rather paradoxical that modern liberals like Ms. Finestone have vigorously rejected those ideals for a kind of culture-is-only-a-T-shirt notion, one which in effect trivializes real culture, forswears any superiority of ideals, and substitutes ethnics for ethics.

British-forged ideals provided a kind of supra-culture that found a natural home in Canada, whose founders, whether English, French, Scots, or German, were resolved to create a single nation (not two, as the myth goes). Their great resolve, as the historian Donald Creighton, author of *Canada's First Century*, put it, "was not the perpetuation of cultural diversity but the establishment of a united nation."

The first ideal was the faith that universals outside and above us all, such as the good, the true, and the beautiful, could serve as a powerful solvent to unify everyone despite the particularities of private culture. Political and social peace would come from encouraging natural self-completion in the search for these things, however unequal might be the practical results. Truth is discovered by individuals, not engineered by governments. That's deep culture, Sheila (though not to liberal liking).

Second, the above can only happen in the context of a Rule of Law, equal for all, that refuses to grant any privilege to racial or cultural differences. The only people in the modern world to have developed such a complex tradition of first principles were the British, who from *Magna Carta* to Blackstone's *Commentaries* forged the common law, democracy, free parliaments, the jury system, habeas corpus, and the presumption of innocence (in deadly opposition to the Roman civil codes of Europe that presume guilt). All this is a framework for the protection of individuals and their civil societies — against governments. A grand culture, I'd say.

While Canada's first experiment under this ideal, embodied in the French reality, has been troublesome, it is important to remember the hopeful founding mood. Just as English Canadians were frightened of the U.S. experiment in democracy that led to civil war, French Canadians were frightened of the half-century of despotism and French terror that dominated European politics. All were united in cherishing the practical wisdom of the English Constitution as the unifying, supracultural vehicle.

Even Québec's motto, "Je me souviens," which is widely thought to indicate a longing for Montcalm, has a poignant origin. It comes from a poem by the architect of the Québec legislature building, Eugene Taché, whose first line seems to have been joined by historical serendipity to his last two lines, to produce: "Je me souviens, que né sous le lys, je fleuris sous la rose" (I remember, that born under the [French] lily, I flourish under the [English] rose). My bet is that French Canadians will keep voting for the culture of the rose.

Third, it was especially the Christian religion that united

and shaped Canada. Close to 90 percent of Canadians —
including the vast majority of Inuit and Native people — continue to declare "Christian" as their faith. Sheila may have no
culture, but deep in the everyday consensus of Canadian
manners and mores is the profound, if unacknowledged,
presence of the spirit and work of Christ, of St. Augustine,
of St. Thomas. Religious culture has been a powerful unifying
force for Canadians, and remains so.

Last, there is the indelibly beautiful and character-
moulding — even heroic — language, literature, art,
and architecture of our Western tradition. Da Vinci,
Michelangelo, Dante, Chaucer, Shakespeare, Milton, Balzac,
Wordsworth, Rodin; Chartres, Westminster, the Louvre;
Beethoven, Handel, Bach; the charitable societies, the great
schools, the universities, all, all sprang from . . . our culture.
It is almost too rich to bear.

Multiculturalism, affirmative action, quotas — all such
flawed policies are a direct attack on our culture, a movement
away from common universal ideals, towards parochial
nationalisms and legal favouritism based on race and blood.

Ms. Finestone has as deep a reason as any to fear her own
philosophy.

WE DO HAVE A CULTURE!

REAL CULTURES ARE NOT necessarily compatible. They are more often than not competitive. Neither is real culture like a T-shirt, to be changed at will. It is part of each of us, profoundly rooted in the concrete experiences of everyday life; in the smell-to-make-you-swoon of the *madeleine* cake, of which Marcel Proust wrote so movingly for the French; in the haunting call of the loon, for me.

And real cultures are also, as one critic put it, either raising or lowering themselves. If you want to know whether your culture is headed up or down, just look to the leaders — the thinkers, teachers, writers, and political visionaries — who will always be on the ramparts first. If they are defending and promoting the core beliefs, you're looking at a rising culture. But if your leaders are the first and most powerful critics of the culture, or simply fail to defend it, or seek to replace it with a patsy policy, then it's headed straight to the bottom.

Lowering cultures are ripe for invasion, and if they are of the mealy-mouthed, everything-goes, modern liberal type, then not much has to be done by the invader. In the way that Marx said capitalists would sell the rope used to hang them with, most modern democracies, so devoted to diversity and pluralism, have failed to defend themselves.

Their weakness is most easily seen in multicultural policy, an abstract idea of culture imposed from the top by modern democratic governments as a desperate ploy to raise up what they have themselves lowered. Such eviscerating policy abstractions erode the real culture and create a vacuum into which some competitive real culture will surely move.

What has been the real culture of Canada? Well, if by culture — as I contend — we must ask what specific kind of people, what religion, what political institutions, what philosophy, what economic system, what literature and art a people live by, then the answer for Canada is easy. And liberals faint when I say this, so I will have to shout.

According to Statistics Canada, our census takers, and any number of respectable polls, we can justly use the word *overwhelming* in its proper sense, to say:

Canada, including all aboriginal and Native people, has only 9 percent visible minorities. That is a coward's way of saying that Canada is an *overwhelmingly* white country in the same way (let's spell it out) that Jamaica, say, is overwhelmingly black, or Japan is overwhelmingly oriental.

An *overwhelming* 80 percent of Canadians say they are Christian, empty pews and all.

Our practical language of commerce, our "public" language, is about 80 to 90 percent English. Canada is *overwhelmingly* an English-speaking nation.

Canada's political institutions — a Senate, a Parliament, a court, democratic elections, personal freedom under a rule of law — remain *overwhelmingly* British in their history, tradition, and design (even in Québec).

Now I submit that these things, especially the love of these things, constitute a deeply satisfying and proud culture, and that our official failure to teach, promote, and fondly protect them will be our undoing, because multiculturalism, which is a policy and not a culture, cannot take their place. So something else will.

Consider the recent court bid by the Islamic Schools Federation of Ontario to allow official Islamic school holidays.

Islam, in its fundamentalist forms, is specifically, even pro-gramatically, anti-Christian. We Christians are unbelievers. Infidels. In Islamic law, conversion out of Islam is a capital offence. No pluralism here. These folks are not fooling around. In an *American Spectator* interview in December of 1993, Hassan Hathout, Ph.D., leader of New Horizons Islamic school in Los Angeles, said, "It is our duty to educate mankind" (the infidels). He shudders "at the [Christian] idea that God took on a human form," and adds that for Muslims, Christianity "is an illness planning to attack us."

Islam also despises democracy as an inferior form of governance that seeks to substitute the shifting will of a majority for the truth as ordained by God and the *Shari'a*, the perfect law of Islam. Accordingly, as one scholar put it, "every major fundamentalist thinker has repudiated popular sovereignty as a rebellion against God, the sole legislator." They are keen "to demonstrate democracy's inferiority to Islamic government." That's why the Islamic faithful say they only need "one man, one vote . . . once" — in order then to govern by Islamic rules. Diversity? Only for multicultural suckers.

Those of pure Islamic faith, according to distinguished historian Bernard Lewis, have a profound contempt for the unbeliever and all his ways. (That's you and me.) For them, "democracy is obviously an irrelevance. They are, however, willing to demand and exploit the opportunities that a self-proclaimed democratic system by its own logic is bound to offer them." Fundamentalist Muslims especially despise the democratic world's egalitarian notion of individual "rights," engraved in egalitarian charters. For them, only God has rights. Humans have duties.

So as a Canadian people with a definable culture, we must decide either to recognize and start raising that culture, or resign ourselves to handing out more of the multicultural rope with which we will surely be hanged.

WHEN POPPIES TRUMP TURBANS

I HAVE BEEN TRYING TO figure out why, ever since the turban turmoil of 1994, each "Remembrance Day" is sadder than the last. I think it's because we've forgotten what to remember.

It strikes me that the 115,000 young Canadians who gave their lives to protect our way of life against top-down rule must now be rolling in their graves.

All the more galling, on Remembrance Day, 1994, were the editorials and columns by smug journalists high on pluralism actually urging readers not to buy a poppy. Some argued the Canadian Legion should "pay the price" for the refusal of some halls to permit the wearing of headgear.

But asking us to choose between poppies, turbans, yarmulkes, and stetsons falsifies a continuing debate.

At the heart of this mess are three misunderstood principles surrounding tolerance, private property, and religious belief, all now under attack by rights-seeking, charter-bearing Sikhs.

Perhaps one day we will awaken to discover that there is an inherent conflict between the idea of "tolerance," and the idea of "rights," because someone who is claiming a right is doing so regardless of whether or not we tolerate the claim. A Sikh asserts a right to wear a turban in a Legion Hall; Legion members assert their right to call their own shots and refuse headgear. There has got to be a loser whose view will not be tolerated.

Most cultures have a time-honoured, tit-for-tat solution to such mutual intolerances: When I am in your house, I do it your way; when you are in my house, you do it my way. Or we don't visit each others' houses. Period. Not bad.

Which brings us to the common-law rules and sanctity of private property, that precious heritage of free societies based on ancient British traditions. Our Charter of Rights and Freedoms does not support the right to private property. But it should, else nothing is safe from rights-seekers. Not the homes, offices, or private lives of Christians, Sikhs, or pagans. Nothing. Legions should be able to require bathing suits on their premises, if they wish. Sikhs may do the same on their own property. Who cares?

I asked a priest of the Shromani Sikh Society in Toronto what would happen if I showed up at his temple with the Charter of Rights and Freedoms, demanding my right to enter wearing shoes, and bare-headed. Horrified, he said, "It is absolutely forbidden! All must take off their shoes and cover their heads as a sign of respect."

So now to religion. Some (not all) Sikhs say the turban is a required item of religious apparel, even though millions of devout Sikhs do not wear a turban, and lots of Sikhs remove the turban when it is convenient to do so. My friend and Indian champion Mr. Singh always removed his turban to run against me in the high hurdles. At any rate, a turban is a strong religious symbol for many. Fine.

So now we have a clash of religious values, because in all Christian societies (at least 80 percent of Canadians say they are Christian), the requirement for a male to remove all head-wear in church, in another's place of worship, in a house, at funerals, when greeting women, and in all solemn places, is firmly rooted in Christian religious practice.

In his first letter to the Corinthians, chapter eleven, St. Paul writes, "For a man indeed ought not to cover his head, forasmuch as he is the image and glory of God." Hat-doffing by males in our society originated as a deep show of respect for God and others and continues as a general sign of respect.

Another forgotten truth is that in every culture in the world, veneration of the dead is the most serious religious matter. Beer and peanuts in a Legion Hall may not be wine and wafer. Nevertheless, a gathering of veterans there, if not a communion, is certainly a kind of community specifically organized around the consecration of the dead who gave their lives in war. The poppy is their blood.

All of which is to say that no one should accept the lazy charge of discrimination, racism, or bigotry that liberals (whose only principle, increasingly, is that anything goes) use to weaken such customs. For these are genuine conflicts rooted in contrary traditions. We all know that the Sikh religion is admirable in many ways (not drinking or smoking, honouring God, etc.), and that Sikhs have been ferocious freedom fighters in the wars between Christian states. They fought to defend rights they are now undermining with other rights. They should not be surprised if one day the police crash through their front door with no warrant to search their homes or temples. (See the pieces in Part IV on our new gun law, Bill C-68.)

The forgotten truth is that Christian nations have their own customs and traditions and, unlike so many other nations, we have worked out effective ways consistent with a free society for dealing with conflicts. It simply will not do to have every minority group in Canada grab the Charter of Rights and Freedoms and march into court whenever they cannot force their way on others.

And remember especially: It is not Canada that has the slavery of bonded labour, religious wars, widow-burning, caste systems, infanticide of female children, and disgusting poverty. It is India, the country most Sikhs came here from. Many of them came to Canada to get away from those very evils. We may have learned things from India in the past. Maybe it is India's turn to learn from us.

SOFTEN THE MIND . . . GRAB THE LAND

THE DRUMS CONTINUE TO beat hard all over North America for Native rights, a code phrase for ambitions to claim vast tracts of land — up to 85 percent of some provinces — that Natives say was wrongly appropriated. Unless it is stopped, millions of us will soon have new landlords, some of them armed with machine-guns. Many of these claims are being settled administratively, or in quiet courtrooms out of the public eye. No public consultation. No opportunity for protest.

What frame of mind could make possible, even thinkable, this legal dislodging of a conquering, settled nation? Could it be that after thirty years of so-called pluralism and diversity, those who understand the true, concentric, and vivifying nature of real culture — such as the Québécois, and Native people — are moving in for the kill on their prostrate Anglo masters? Believe it.

In part, this flood of tax-funded claims has been created with the help of ecology-minded liberal lawyers who seek forcibly to recreate what they imagine was a superior, more "spiritual" communal society ruined by nasty Europeans when, with their evil sense of private property, they stomped on all those peaceful, happy, sharing Indian tribes.

But as Brian Lee Crowley explains in his book *Road to Equity*, this is a myth that happens to blend nicely with the post-1960s middle-class fantasy of "living in accord with nature, away from city, factory and office, being able to share rather than compete, enjoying a way of life in common with their fellows." Stewart Brand, an environmental catastrophist in the obvious grip of a death wish, actually wrote in *Whole Earth Catalogue*, "We have wished, we eco-freaks, for a disaster or for social change to bomb us into the stone age, where we might live like Indians in our valley . . . guilt free at last." Indians, guilt free?

For a sobering education on some of the all too familiar human foibles of Native peoples of the world, including their practices of infanticide, wife abuse, torture, human sacrifice, cannibalism, and slavery, read UCLA professor Robert Edgerton's *Sick Societies*. It certainly comes as a shock that many tribes such as the California Chumash, and the Kwakiutl of British Columbia, kept, traded, and often ate, large numbers of slaves.

Most Natives had a well-defined sense of property, harsh laws against theft, and kept a whole warring class to protect their well-defined territory. And Native groups such as the

Five Nations of the Iroquois did a lot of subduing of their own. In *The Iroquois Book of the Great Law* (1916) by A. C. Parker we read that their approved method for forging what they cheerfully termed "The Great Peace" of the Iroquois was to visit all non-conforming tribes and "club the chief to death." In this manner, writes Parker, "every rebellious tribe or nation, almost without exception, was either exterminated or absorbed." It was plain old massacre.

Such confusion is likely why Chief Justice Allan McEachern ruled in 1991 that all aboriginal property rights, even if they ever existed, were "extinguished" at the time of settlement by Europeans. This is what most of us would conclude is the normal aftermath of any conquest. But other judges have disagreed, arguing for two equal sets of rights. However, no federal system can exist that encourages equal authorities for competing rights to its lands, for this unleashes a domino effect of dangerous consequences (as the Cree and Inuit reminded us during the Québec referendum of 1995!).

The hidden disaster behind the Native-rights ruse, however, is that hundreds of thousands of Native citizens — women in particular — are going to be re-subjected to a new and oppressive radical tribalism camouflaged under self-government, against which they will have no meaningful appeal. For the general public, this gets buried by Indo-babblers who say the Native concept of ownership is simply incompatible with "Eurocentric" Western assumptions.

So a lot of gaga modernists and New Agers are busily promoting Nativist theology. Typical was the summer of 1993, on Canada Day, when the *Toronto Star* ran a special section called "Earth Spirit Day," showing a full-dress brave in front of his teepee inviting other Canadians to participate in "Earth Worship." We were asked to worship stones, lakes, and trees, not God as the Creator of these lesser things. This is old paganism resurgent, a direct assault on the Judeo-Christian worldview. Soften the mind before you grab the land.

On a recent bicycle trip around Ontario's beautiful Muskoka area, I saw the Mohawk flag flying over a number of houses. The official road signs that used to say "Mohawk Reserve," now say "Mohawk Territory." Well, this might be a lot easier to accept if it weren't that Canada's 400,000+ Natives (projected to be 700,000 by the year 2070) are among the most highly subsidized people on earth, currently enjoying $5.5 billion — about $15,000 per capita — from the public coffers every year.

There is something repugnant about the idea of financing our own internal takeover. Without any permission asked, in May 1993 Canadians quietly surrendered their sovereignty over a million square miles of their own northland — now renamed Nunavut — to 15,000 Inuit people, who will have their own government, living in what *Vancouver Sun* columnist Trevor Lautens aptly described as "Affirmative Apartheid."

Write to your Member of Parliament. Say you want nunavut.

PORN DESTROYS
WHAT IS GOOD

NAKED CHILDREN DEPICTED strad-
dling excited men in our galleries of high art? Bookstore
shelves creaking with titillating tomes? Every hotel room in
the nation converted to a private porn parlour at the flick of a
switch? What in the world is going on?

Nobody's telling. Canada says the test of obscenity is no
longer "community standards" but, rather, a "harm-based"
test. This new, feminist-inspired definition says something is
obscene if it portrays sexual violence, or degrading or dehu-
manizing acts, or contains the sexual depiction of children.
It seems we have retreated over time from a traditional test
based on harm to society as a whole, to a test based only on
what we judge harmful to individuals.

This is perfectly in keeping with the unwinding of modern

democracy. Just as we have surrendered local control over our own economic lives and futures (high taxes, unfunded pensions, bankrupt welfare systems), our own health care (socialized medicine we cannot afford), and the education of our children (radical curricula in public schools), so have we surrendered our community ability to control sexual smut.

And let us dismiss at once the ridiculous liberal conceit that because social scientists cannot find "proof," porn does not lead to crime or violence. For as Irving Kristol has pointed out, it is "the very same people who seem convinced that advertisements in magazines or displays of violence on television do indeed have the power to corrupt" who deny (usually in the name of free speech) that porn also corrupts. He pointedly adds, "If you believe that no one was ever corrupted by a book, you also have to believe that no one was ever improved by a book (or a play or a movie). No one, not even a university professor, really believes that."

As for the porn/crime/violence connection? Pornography is itself largely a product of a multibillion-dollar international crime industry with vast underground and drug-ring tentacles. It is more appealing when it is forbidden. So whenever it becomes less forbidden, pornographers simply seek out new and kinkier variations another small step beyond the law.

But the most profound spillover effect of pornography is not that it does harm to individuals (don't forget, lots of women are willing porn models and consumers), but to human society as a whole, because it strives ceaselessly to change our concept of what is sexually good.

It does this by promoting a generalized, self-indulgent sexual appetite — sexual feeling for its own sake — as a substitute for and preference to interpersonal human desire and love. And that is likely why, in their inarticulate wisdom, all human societies have banned pornography.

They know instinctively that it is not the prohibition of pornography that "infantilizes us," as one feminist recently (and wrongly) put it. Pornography itself infantilizes. Through the lure of the forbidden, it seeks to turn us away from real human beings towards fantasy and grotesquerie without limits or control. It thus prevents growth and debases society. After all, society needs healthy men and women who seek the demanding joys of love and family, not millions of leering, masturbating citizens.

The proof of this is in the porn pudding. Billions of dollars change hands. Film schools the world over spew out eager graduates. The camera arts have never been more sophisticated. Yet anyone exposed to a pornographic movie must surely have wondered how it could be so aesthetically awful.

Obviously, there is some reason why it is impossible, not to make, but to sell, a work of pornography with high aesthetic standards, intriguing dialogue, and compelling narrative. Surely it's because these three elements always threaten to lift the consumer above the merely sensual, and introduce the possibility of judgement — on others, and on oneself. Judgement means guilt may quickly follow. No thanks, is the response.

Pornography is therefore trapped, between aesthetic limits it cannot broach at the top, and the boredom caused by repetitive, raw sensuality at the bottom, a boredom it must always attempt to escape through novelty and variation. That is why pornography always develops unidirectionally, towards the more violent and kinky, and never towards the more beautiful. As tolerance is raised, porn must further lower itself, ultimately embracing the sexualization of death, as it did in live stage killings in ancient times to the roar of insatiable crowds, and as it does in snuff videos now.

In 1992, British police smashed an international porn-video ring selling thousands of titles such as *Cannibal Holocaust*, *Human Experiments*, and *Blood-Sucking Freaks*. One apparently showed an excited man who murdered a pregnant woman by slicing open her belly and eating her baby. Clearly, the Roman amphitheatre has entered the modern living room.

No, the danger to society is not pornography itself, but the normalization of pornography. In a traditional society, porn cannot be normalized because parents who demand close control over what influences their children will march on the corner store, pitchforks in hand. But to do the same today, they have to march all the way to Ottawa and face a Charter that has disempowered their community.

So the solution? Every community in the country must pass tough anti-porn laws and then march as a group against Ottawa and the Charter, legal pitchforks in hand.

WHY SHOULD THE CHARTER PROTECT APPETITES?

T HERE ARE FEW SPECTACLES quite as riveting and pitiable as a revved-up politician pursuing a false idea in the name of equality. One gets the sense that the snake has charmed the charmer. One of Justice Minister Allan Rock's pet snakes is the idea of homosexual rights, and "All shall be the same in this society" is the tune that charms.

I would argue, rather, that unless we maintain our historical distinction between individual rights and social rights, there will be no society left. All citizens of Canada, including all homosexuals, already have the same, exactly equal, individual rights (freedom of speech, right to trial, and so on). But not everyone has, nor ought they to have, the same social rights. Simply being a citizen is sufficient to get all individual rights. But in a normal society, a citizen must qualify for specified social rights and benefits, and society has the prerogative of stipulating exactly how, rigorously excluding — that is, discriminating against — unqualified individuals.

For example, you cannot have a Canada Pension until you reach a certain age (unless you are an MP — then age doesn't matter!). Nor can you have Social Assistance unless you demonstrate difficult circumstances. Nor can you qualify for veteran payments unless you have fought for Canada in a war. Nor are you a legal adult until a specified age. *And,* most importantly, you can't have the legal or tax benefits of a spouse unless you marry someone of the opposite sex.

But Mr. Rock seems to believe that qualification for social rights is unnecessary. So my phone has been ringing with calls from distraught Members of Parliament who say there is a damnable new Charter argument designed to get social rights for homosexuals.

Most people have insisted the Charter should only protect against discrimination based on immutable characteristics such as colour, ethnicity, and gender, but never behaviour. But the new argument says: How about religion? Religion is protected, and that's not immutable! Unfair!

But there is an unbridgeable gap between these two. For starters, religion underpins Canada's Charter of Rights and Freedoms, the preamble of which specifically states: "Canada is founded upon principles that recognize the supremacy of God." Homosexuality is not mentioned as a principle upon which Canada is founded (yet). A Charter would be Orwellian if it did not protect from discrimination those who believe in its own founding principle.

Religion is universal. It infuses all societies, and directly or indirectly shapes their collective identity. But homosexuality is the opposite. It is a widely spurned behaviour, even a counter-identity, practised by only 1.5 to 2 percent of the population in most nations.

Religion, though fallible like all things human, at least promotes moral behaviour through the worship of God, the highest Good. Homosexuality is the opposite. If not outlawed by most countries, it is deemed morally wrong, or sinful, by overwhelming majorities of normal people — even by those who defend the legal right to practise it privately. Charters and human-rights codes should not be used to protect behaviours universally deemed bad.

Religion promotes procreation. It is supportive of society, traditional family, and the continuation of both. Homosexuality is the opposite. Two homosexuals cannot procreate with each other. A fully homosexual society would self-destruct. Charters should protect procreation and pass over in silence other choices made by free individuals.

Religion is healthy, too. Societies that stress sincere religious beliefs tend to be the lowest in sociopathology, alcohol abuse, and crime. Homosexuality is the opposite. It is unhealthy, even dangerous behaviour. Homosexuals die younger, and have vastly more social, psychological, sexual, alcohol, and drug problems than any other group. About 90 percent of all AIDS deaths in Canada and the U.S. are of male homosexuals.

Religion is culturally inherited. The vast majority of the world's children are inducted into their religion before adulthood, and never change. In this sense, religion is in theory mutable, but is in practice only quasi-mutable.

Homosexuality is the opposite. No one, no parent, no community leader, no one except another (usually older) homosexual would ever voluntarily induct a child into homosexuality. About half of all homosexuals themselves even say they would "become upset" if a child of theirs became homosexual (Bell and Weinberg). And despite feverish attempts to prove otherwise, in no sense is homosexual behaviour immutable, as is skin colour, or ethnicity. The respected sexologists Masters and Johnson have repeatedly shown recovery rates of 70 percent for homosexuals.

Religion is necessarily based on spiritual belief, but not necessarily on behaviour. Homosexuality is the opposite. No beliefs are required. What is required to identify and define homosexuality is an act. Without homosexual behaviour, there is no homosexuality to worry about, and this fact alone is sufficient grounds to deny protection.

Charters should not protect or promote the mere appetites or behaviours of any individual or group.

Over to you, Mr. Minister.

A FEVERISH SEARCH
FOR "EQUALITY"

Recently a group of maverick law students (moderately conservative, that is) at Queen's University, Kingston, invited me to debate Sheila McIntyre, one of Canada's front-line feminist law professors, who is openly dedicated to the destruction of our ordinary concept of the law. The sparks were flying before an overflow crowd.

Professor McIntyre argued that the differences between people and groups in society are not natural, circumstantial, or deserved in any way; that "systemic" oppression exists throughout society. She wants the law, therefore, to create true equality by treating people differentially: by handicapping those with power and bestowing advantages on those without.

She wants lawyers, judges, and MPs to be social engineers. However, the normal concept of law in the West has always struggled against such activists to insist that all people, rich or poor, smart or stupid, strong or weak, without distinction, must submit equally to the same Rule of Law; that by and large, despite natural or circumstantial inequalities, this is more fair.

But Marxists and radicals like McIntyre joke that a free society under this merely "formal law" concept just means the rich and the poor alike are allowed to sleep under park benches. Formal law, they argue, can produce only "formal equality," as distinct from "substantive," or concrete, equality, under which everyone would have the same material advantages. They are quite willing to surrender their freedom to a massive egalitarian state to gain this extreme sort of equality.

Freedom-lovers rebut that if the law is anything besides formal, then it is not law at all. It has been transformed into politics. They believe freedom is more important than equality and the best kind of law is therefore prohibitive: law that simply tells you what you cannot do, but which otherwise leaves you alone and free.

There is real danger, however, in switching from formal to substantive law, because throughout history, whenever the law gets seized by social activists (who may themselves have good, if misguided motives), it soon thereafter gets captured by much stronger political activists who quickly shove the softer McIntyre types aside. Then, in the absence of formal safeguards, anyone may quickly become its victims. So may the ideologues themselves.

In fact, most egalitarian revolutions that rely on substantive laws to achieve their extreme political purposes soon devour their intellectual founders, seen to lack stomach for real blood.

That's how Robespierre, the radical egalitarian theorist of the French Revolution, the "prophet of virtue" who had ordered thousands of his own citizens guillotined, got killed in the name of liberty: there was no formal law, or procedure, left to protect him.

By then, the laws are primarily imperative: laws that order you around and make you live a certain way, or do certain specific things to fulfil utopian ideals, creating advantages for some and penalties for others in a feverish quest for equality. Canada has many such "equity"-type laws now, created by all sorts of "tribunals."

There was some pleasure to be had in reminding Professor McIntyre that it was she who had an $80,000-a-year job as a tenured professor and could not be fired. It was she who was the former president of LEAF (Legal Education and Action Fund), a radical feminist group supported by massive government grants that has already radicalized our society through just such changes in the law as she proposes. And it is she who gets her turgid articles published in state-subsidized journals. So, in fact, she is herself a power-broker and stakeholder and exerts her own brand of influence over those who prefer a free society to a tyrannical one.

Just after this debate, writer Rob Martin published an article in *Lawyers Weekly* citing the dean of the law school, Donald McCrae, who said, "The idea of equity is that everyone should get the same advantage." What a riot. It has apparently never occurred to the good dean that at such a point the whole concept of advantage has no meaning.

So Queen's invented a "discretionary" admissions policy, justified by the argument that academic admissions standards are a social evil (that is, systemically oppressive). The policy stipulates that up to 30 percent of all those admitted to the first year of law studies may be admitted with below-standard marks.

In addition, because many of these inferior students will not do well on exams, Queen's offers them "examination accommodation" (they can have twice the allotted time to write their exams).

After one year of this policy, however, it was discovered that more than half the students who applied for and received such accommodation were in fact not members of any minority group. So to solve this new problem the "Equity Committee" recommended that *all* students be granted such accommodation. Lowering standards for all is how equality is to be gained. This is "substantive" law at work.

I wonder if these new lawyers, once graduated, will allow us "billing accommodation" should we mistakenly engage their services?

III

SEPARATION ANXIETIES

The last shot in the preservation
of British rule will be fired by a French-Canadian.

— ETIENNE TACHÉ, A FOUNDING FATHER OF CANADIAN CONFEDERATION,
DEFENDING THE EXCELLENCE OF THE BRITISH CONSTITUTIONAL
FRAMEWORK FOR CANADA, 1865

HELL, NO! QUÉBEC CAN'T GO

In mid-1994, sly Jacques Parizeau, leader of a small provincial party, launched a revolutionary campaign aimed at the radical dismemberment of this nation of twenty-seven million people.

Somebody pinch me. Here was a campaign that ran contrary to the will of the Canadian people, the Senate, the House of Commons, at least nine provincial legislatures — even (according to the polls) to the will of Parizeau's own electorate! Worst of all, perhaps, it was a campaign that openly mocked the constitutional laws of Canada. Yet there was little national reaction to his preposterous scheme. Mostly invisible leaders, and a rattled press.

Now, another Québec referendum later, and with another likely to come soon, it's time we had straight answers to straight questions. At the least, it's time the tail stopped wagging the dog.

QUESTION: WHO GIVES PERMISSION TO SEPARATE?

In a recent heated radio debate against Bernard Landry, vice-president of the Parti Québécois, I asked, "Why do you think Québec, or any other province, has the right to separate?"

Landry blurted out: "Democracy. We have been a democracy for three hundred years!" He cited Parizeau's tiresome slogan that all a separatist party needs is a vote of "a majority of 50 percent plus one."

His eyes glazed over in the studio when I argued that this was neither legal nor sensible, for it means that if fully one-half of the people says, No, and one-half says, Yes — meaning both sides are legitimately opposed, balanced, and equally right — a single citizen could walk into a ballot box and decide the entire destiny of Canada. I did not know at the time that the Québec referendum of 1995 would almost come down to exactly that, with the separatists barely one percentage point away from "victory."

Fortunately, Canada is a federal state, and not a simple democracy. It is, if anything, a constitutional democracy. The core idea of federations is that they have a tangible and legal reality that is more than the sum of their parts. As constitutional lawyer Stephen Scott of McGill has said, it would be "disastrous for constitutional negotiations to proceed on the premise that a province, if dissatisfied, can overthrow the state." No federation could possibly survive under such conditions. In federations, all serious matters are decided not by the opinion of one-half of any political party, or group or province, but by the whole nation according to the law of the constitution. Both Parizeau and Lucien Bouchard (former Leader of Her Majesty's Disloyal Opposition) know very well that Canada's Constitution already has a perfectly good legal amending procedure (in Part V) that could be used to permit the separation of any province if the people *as a whole* wanted such a thing.

So the straight answer is: No province of Canada has the legal right to separate without the consent of the House of Commons, the Senate, and at least seven if not all of the provincial legislatures. Any other method constitutes a revolt against the government of Canada.

QUESTION: WHO DECIDES WHAT CAN BE TAKEN?

Canada as a whole belongs to the people as a whole, regardless of where they happen to live. It's like a residence owned in common by ten people. Someone trying to rip a province out of Canada is like one of the ten chain-sawing a room off the common residence. Only one may live there, but the room belongs to all. It so happens that most of Canada's territory inside Québec's boundaries was originally placed under Québec's jurisdiction to be administered as a province of Canada, not as a separate nation. Canada would rightfully reclaim it.

So the straight answer is: Canadians, through their government, alone have the right to decide on all terms and conditions for the break-up of Canada, on debt repayment, or on land settlement, under the law of the Constitution of Canada.

QUESTION: CAN WE SEPARATE FROM SEPARATISTS?

This is a catch-22, because any argument used to legitimize the division of Canada can as easily be used to legitimize the division of the maverick province. In Québec, Native people and the Inuit, as we saw just before the 1995 referendum, quickly seized upon separatist-style arguments to remain in Canada. One Anglo group has campaigned to form Québec West if Québec separates. Only force can stop such a domino effect.

So the straight answer is: Tit for tat.

There it is, frère Jacques — and frère Lucien. Under the laws of Canada, there can be: No unilateral referendum. No illegal separation. No taking territory from Canada. No indivisible new country.

Are our political leaders so fearful of losing votes in Québec that they put their careers ahead of their country?

Courage, I say. It's past time to demand an explicit and unequivocal public statement from all separatists that they will seek their objectives strictly under the constitutional laws of Canada.

Their fellow Canadians expect nothing less.

THE SEPARATION KID

In the lead-up to their 1995 referendum campaign, Québec separatists behaved like frustrated promoters of an upcoming boxing match with only one declared contestant. Things had been under preparation for too long, and big money was at stake. Lenders were nervous, and the Separation Kid had lost his only fight years ago.

Yet he was back with a vengeance, helped into the ring by new friends and beefed up with heavy-duty steroids. Victory was said to be certain. But spotlights shone dim on an empty white mat, and sleepy journalists struggled to stay awake through the face-saving hype from greasy organizers. Something was wrong.

Part of the problem seems to have been that there was no referee. And most important, no one could figure out exactly who the mystery opponent in the other corner would be. So an uncertain public stayed away to enjoy the summer, keeping tabs on the hype between their burgers and beer. Maybe they would catch the action on cable in the fall.

Well, advance sales picked up real fast when the news got out that the guy in the other corner was not the expected opponent from Québec but (shock of shocks) an import! A foreigner!

Preceded by a horrific roar, out of the spotlit tunnel, draped in a huge white and red flag, came a confident bruiser with arms like a gorilla, the words "ROC" stamped across his back. It was . . . the Rest Of Canada.

More terrible for the suddenly trembling separatists, into the ring jumped the official referee. Not the easy-to-deceive (maybe even to bribe) Danny the Democrat, as expected. As positively counted on. But, yikes! The worst imaginable ref. A fair one. Who knew the rules. It was Constitutional Carl, wearing flashy red and white Supreme Court robes. Suddenly, all seats were filled. The fight was on.

And that's the way it should be.

But for some reason, it didn't happen that way during the referendum, and doesn't look like it will in future scraps, either.

For some reason, Canadians persist in the frustrating and illusory belief that the separation of Québec, or any other province, is a solely provincial decision. That by some democratic right, any province, anytime, can call a fight and knock out Canada.

But from what, exactly, springs this idea, or, rather, this belief? Has it simply slipped through, veiled in rank laziness, unobserved? Faced with a dire, even treasonous assault on this fair and just Dominion by the spirit of Montcalm, will Canadians continue to slumber?

Or could it be, as Churchill put it, that you can fool some of the people all the time, all of them some of the time, but not all of them all the time? If so, then what a relief. Maybe Canadians are not fooled. Maybe they are supremely knowledgeable and confident. Maybe they know it's beer and burgers until the real fight begins, then we'll see, eh? Maybe they have known all along who the real oppponent, and the real ref, are (chuckle, chuckle). So why talk about it?

Centuries ago, Italian nobles called this attitude "sprezzatura." This admiring word was used to describe any difficult achievement performed with an appearance of ease. Even if some challenge was complex and impossibly difficult, no real gentleman, no self-possessed man or woman, should ever let on. Self-control and personal poise were the thing. Honour, skill, and grace under fire.

So that's it. Canadians lingering over barbecue smoke between these recurring fights are really just latter-day nobles supremely confident of their grip on what it means to be a nation. No need to think about a response just yet. The right action will flow naturally from sound reasoning at the right time.

Maybe they are also firmly aware that people of sound mind do not create corporations whose subsidiaries have rights to destroy the parent organization. Maybe they know that even a school soccer team cannot function if a single player decides to break mutually agreed rules. Maybe they know that any agreement to join two or more parties, whether in marriage, business, or politics, requires open recognition of binding rules superior to the parties themselves.

Alas, many fear the truth lies elsewhere. That the ROC does not even know there is a fight, so he is unprepared, lacks self-esteem, and — far more damaging — is out of shape. That Constitutional Carl has gotten sidetracked in a bar on the way to the arena (just what those clever fight organizers were counting on). And that with ROC sidetracked, and Carl otherwise deployed, the secret plan of the separatists has always been to put a straw man in the other corner, then put Democratic Dan through correctness classes until he comes up with the right decision.

They figure even if the Separation Kid loses this time, it will be a victory of sorts. He was just practising, after all. And most of all, they know that this fight, win or lose, will at least establish the principle — nowhere to be found in the history of Canada, or of any federation that has ever existed — that any province can call a fight, set the rules, and try to dissolve the whole. So break out the champagne, they cry. Our opponents will pay for it, forever, and we can demand a rematch as soon as the Kid is better trained.

ONE LOUSY VOTE . . . EVERYONE'S DESTINY

THE EXPERTS CONTINUE to quarrel openly over the situation in Québec, a signal to the public that no one knows what in hell is going on, though everyone has a growing fear that hell is where we'll end up. For ordinary Canadians, it seems the high principle of "democracy," which they defend passionately, is being used to dismember their beloved country — which they also defend passionately.

Now for driving back intrusive governments, direct democracy is a good thing. But using it to break up a constitutional federation is another matter. And so it is curious that the democracy thing has become such a panacea notion in modern Canada — and the U.S. — because the founders of both nations designed governments specifically to check its influence.

Most of them, as Harvard historian Bernard Bailyn puts it,

considered democracy "a word that denoted the lowest order of society . . . generally associated with the threat of civil disorder and the early assumption of power by a dictator."

Goethe warned Europeans that "there is nothing more odious than the majority; for it consists of a few powerful leaders, a certain number of accommodating scoundrels and subservient weaklings, and a mass of men who trudge after them without in the least knowing their own minds." And James Madison, an architect of the American Constitution, put it most poignantly when he warned that direct democracies "have ever been spectacles of turbulence and contention; have ever been found incompatible with personal security or the rights of property; and have in general been as short in their lives as they have been violent in their deaths."

When we keep in mind that surveys of the voting public reveal a grade seven intellectual level, the fear of democracy is more readily understood, for only a minority of any society is ever successful enough to accumulate significant property, generate wealth, or lead wisely.

Thus a system of "majority rule" (50 percent plus one vote) soon becomes a licence for the majority to plunder the successful minority through exercise of the political means, instead of seeking its own wealth through the more difficult productive means: so they vote massively for taxation and redistribution. Arguably, this has happened in Canada with a vengeance over the past thirty years, and our blind binge of public spending proves it. The great bulk of Canada's so-called social spending is transferred to middle-income Canadians.

The main side-effect of this vast internal redistributive

empire has been the frantic creation of policies designed to homogenize Canada, even against its natural heterogeneity. Ye shall be one! Yet it is difficult to refer to all this as the progress, or development, of democracy. Those terms imply a movement towards a better stage, and a faith that if we just invoke "democracy" often enough, then by mere incantation, justice and peace will follow in its wake. That is the way the word is being used by the Parti Québécois.

But this is a shaky faith indeed. It is surely more accurate to refer to the unwinding of democracy, a term implying that the whole process may have a life of its own, and is taking us to places we don't necessarily wish to go.

For example, it has been the imposition of our homogenizing democratic empire, ostensibly designed to pacify and incorporate all the people of Canada, against which the Parti Québécois faithful vociferously strain. Which is to say that we may hear too late the warnings of our forefathers as to how the simplistic concept of "50 percent plus one" can ruin a nation. How, on this basis, as a recent *Globe and Mail* editorial put it, "it will take fewer than two million votes to effectively sunder the Dominion of Canada" — about 10 percent of the voting population.

It was precisely to avoid this sort of possibility that Canada's original Constitution, the BNA Act, never made provision for any legal dismemberment, and that the Charter of 1982 says that Canada cannot be put asunder except by the highest institutions and authorities in the land, representing all the people.

But never by the rabble. And certainly never by any tinpot political general leading a small, misinformed, radicalized (and racialized) minority into some confused future utopia after enjoying a century of national largesse.

Pundits everywhere warn that to insist on such "legalism" is frivolous. That some mysterious, unofficial democratic right of the Parti Québécois to sunder Canada must be respected.

But it bears repeating that such unfettered democracy, applied only to a part of the democratic whole, is the ultimate legalism, for it argues that if two sides in the part are equally balanced, and therefore equally legitimate, one anonymous citizen with a grade seven education, from a fractious minority, in a single province, carries in his or her person the legal right to walk into a ballot box and change the destiny of the whole forever.

We have been warned by our founders that great nations are made of sterner stuff.

STOMPIN' TOM
PUT IT BEST

Big GUY SLUGS LITTLE guy? "Unfair!" is the universal cry. Yet, in a simple democracy, when the majority squishes the minority, we somehow deem it fair.

Fine. But that gives zero protection to the 49 percent left behind. So various sorts of constitutional democracy, such as we find in Canada, the U.S., Germany, and elsewhere, were designed to provide equal legal protection of rights and property for all the people. But such guarantees obviously mean nothing without the primal constitutional integrity of the federation itself. Who else would protect minorities such as the 3.4 million Canadians who would have been abandoned to Québec had the Yes vote won in the 1995 referendum?

I hope we have learned that if our primal national commitments are forgotten, or simply undefended by the people and their leaders, then in an ironic flip the majority becomes exposed to a reverse tyranny — of the minority! Little guy slugs big guy. And a nasty little guy, to boot, willing to lie and cheat.

Democracy falls victim to this process of self-immolation whenever its fetishistic affection for simple democracy permits majorities in a part, to be used against the constitutional democracy of the whole people, giving rise — as the Cree and Inuit have demonstrated with forceful timing — to a never-ending sequence of democratically justified divisions and territorial claims.

What our leaders must therefore enunciate is the reality Abraham Lincoln taught America at the end of sword and musket: that there is a fundamental conflict between simple democratic theory, and the theory of democratic federation. Once states are constituted by or agree to join a federation, they effectively surrender their sovereignty to the larger whole; a sovereignty that can only be transferred back to them by agreement of the whole (or taken back unilaterally, by revolution). Democratic methods, when used by a part as a political weapon to dismember the democratic whole, must be declared illegitimate.

In the run-up to Québec's sculduggerous, Maybe Referendum (maybe separation, maybe sovereignty-association, maybe partnership, maybe Canadian dollars, maybe passports, maybe MPs, and so on), millions of Canadians gave passionate voice to their rising feelings of anger at the betrayal of our federation.

Stompin' Tom Connors put it best in the *Toronto Star*, when he said it was a cryin' shame "that a handful of Canadians is allowed to decide the fate of Canada." I submit that no single Canadian leader or politician has put the case more forcefully than Tom. It was indeed a handful (barely 10 percent of the eligible voters of Canada). And this minority (a quarter of whom actually believed they could separate from Canada and still send us Members of Parliament!) was truly being allowed to hold a referendum (on a shamelessly deceitful question) by cowardly, spineless politicians and courts and a feckless media frightened to stand up for the integrity of this great nation.

But the name of the game has changed drastically. Millions of sleepwalking Canadians got a hair-raising referendum jolt they will not soon forget. As a result, we have a new class of radicals in Canada. They are called citizens. Citizens refreshingly surprised and moved by their own patriotism. So my guess is that it's game over for simple democratic separatism.

Any separation of any parts of Canada in the future will have to be constitutional, arranged by the people as a whole. All we need is a little more confidence in our founding principles — and Stompin' Tom for Prime Minister.

Meanwhile, Canada remains an irony inside a conundrum. For two generations, the rest of Canada has swallowed the multicultural myth and cheerfully forgotten its history and traditions in the name of pan-liberal diversity and pluralism. As a result, as Sheila Finestone, Minister of Multiculturalism, has proudly reminded us, "Canada has no national culture."

But Québec, while always accepting the multicult publicly, fought it privately every step of the way, struggling fanatically to preserve every scrap of French identity, singing songs of blood and soil, even unto punishing merchants for daring to print English letters larger than French ones on commercial signs.

So, in a delicious irony, the "ethnics" Parizeau thinks sunk his leaky ship (though it was really his own francophones who failed him), these very same ethnics who have in fact partaken in the dilution of the English culture of the Rest of Canada, have ended up saving Canada — simply because it was too weak to save itself!

Now this is a welcome, but quite insufficient, broth to nourish us. If Canada feels any will to survive as a civic state (as opposed to a religious, cultural, or ethnic state), it had better start expressing this will.

We need a declaration from the prime minister and all premiers on the first civic law of all: that Canada is a duly constituted federation with a duty to protect all the people. Any change in our democratic rights, or Canada's duties, can only be with the express sanction of all the people. Any province wishing to separate must seek secession only under the laws of Canada, based on a provincial special majority of at least two-thirds, on a clear and unambiguous question, followed by approval of terms, by the same two-thirds measure of all the people of Canada.

IV

IT'S A CRIME

Without justice there are but litigants —
the oppressors and the victims.

— NAPOLEON

DOSTOEVSKY'S QUIVERING TAIL

 T HE HUNT IS ON — it has never stopped — for criminal genes, nifty neurons, and classy chemicals that will make us perfect, or at least explain why we are not.

In his great novel *The Brothers Karamazov* (1880), Dostoevsky's central character, Ivan, the brother who pushes reason to its limit, finally concludes that if God is dead, "everything is permitted." If there is no ultimate good in the universe against which to measure our behaviour, then men will decide for themselves what is good.

By the end of the nineteenth century, in the hands of the German philosopher Friedrich Nietzsche, this idea of creating our own standard of good — making ourselves perfect — became the philosophy of the Superman, the heroic individual who shapes the world through his own will and thus lives beyond good and evil. (Apologists for Hitler's Naziism relied on such thinking to deplore Christianity as a slave religion, because it preaches the imperfection of man and requires obedience to a moral code that protects the weak.)

It happened that one of the most famous scientists in Europe at the same time was the Frenchman Claude Bernard, whose experiments held hope, for those toiling in the aftermath of Darwinism, of some material explanation for human behaviour that would do away with the need for God altogether. Man would be made perfect by science.

Dostoevsky mocks this notion through Ivan's colourful pagan brother, Dimitri, whose thoughts are a parody of our modern Human Genome Project — that ultimate scientific safari in search of the genetic god within:

"Well, imagine: the nerves in the head. I mean the nerves in the brain . . . have sort of little tails, and, well, as soon as the little tails of those nerves begin to quiver . . . an image appears . . . that is, an object or an event. That's why I contemplate and then think — because of the little tails and not at all because I have a soul . . . science is a wonderful thing! A new man is coming."

What Dostoevsky ridiculed was physical determinism: the emerging notion — essential to atheists — that everything we are results from an unbroken sequence of physical events beyond our control, starting with the smallest, the quivering little tail or gene or atom.

It is important to connect the two conclusions (everything is permitted; our actions arise from little tails) to the consequent idea that everything must also be forgiven. After all, those who live beyond good and evil do not want a conscience.

Those whose actions are determined do not need one. If it's all in the genes, or in Prozac, or Ritalin, or the hypothalamus, then, indeed, all can be forgiven . . . can't it? The poet T. S. Eliot explained this urge best when he wrote that such moral utopians are "dreaming of systems so perfect that no one will need to be good."

Meanwhile, the great embarrassment is that our modern liberal democracies have lavished more money on murderers, thieves, assaulters, rapists, teen pregnancies, runaway husbands, illegitimate births, drug and sex abusers, and pedophiles (all of whom have offended against morality) than has been spent on their likes in the whole prior history of the world, only to produce vastly more of these things! Lavishing money on immoral behaviour creates as much of it as we care to tolerate.

For the whole ancient pagan era, fate, issuing from the capriciousness of the gods, was fingered as the ultimate cause of wins or woes. Our destiny was something decided outside ourselves, only vaguely decipherable from the mysterious warnings of oracles, by the reading of entrails, or by tearing out the beating hearts of sacrificed maidens.

What postmodern, cutting-edge scientists are really searching for is no longer a social or economic cause — a fate — outside us, but a new, jazzed-up, quivering little tail. A fate inside us. Not the mere sign of evil, but the evil thing itself. Then they will medicate, excise, or redesign the evil. They will exert the will to create the Superman, free at last from the need to be good.

The strange paradox is that what has distinguished the Christian ethos for two millennia is its repudiation of many capricious gods for one perfect God. It is man who is imperfect, and human evil comes not from fate but from misuse of the human will, from inside ourselves, in a directly controllable inner spiritual form. All individuals, rich and poor alike, are equal in their capacity for moral agency. Human evil is not a thing, nor caused by a thing, whether a pagan god, or a little tail. On this precept was built the glory of Western law and civilization.

What the scientists fail to see is that while chemicals or lobotomies may alter our moods, this does not mean we have to engage in particular behaviours. Moods and feelings themselves are intransitive. They require no necessary object or action until, in a moment of choice, we decide on one. And all such decisions are based on values.

In a fit of depression or anger a man may decide to satisfy his mood by killing someone or, more hopefully, by going for a run. Or maybe by resolving his anger and learning about love.

Our moods and passions may not always be free, but our decisions are — even the decision to enslave ourselves to our moods and passions.

GENDER BASHING HURTS US ALL

THE WORST WAR OF ALL, said G. K. Chesterton, is the war between the sexes. That is because we are all born of a mother and begotten by a father. This mother-father-child triangle is a universal of human experience. Even those with dead or absent parents live forever with the presence of the absence, so to speak. When governments founder, economies collapse, or wars devastate, this indelible community of men, women, and children is all we have.

So it is all the sadder every December to see the feverish grasping for exaggerated claims by a stupefied media and crass activists, eager to convert the sadness of the 1989 Lepine slaughter of fourteen female students into a national male-hating enterprise. Women were urged to indulge in a "march of rage and mourning," as part of a program to combat "violence against women."

Let us be clear. Marc Lepine was a nut. Whatever he believed, for us to insist he slaughtered gender diminishes his crime. Those girls were full human beings, and his was the highest crime. It is their humanity, not their gender, we must remember, and in remembering, save them from any foul, narrow motive — and from politics.

Feminists argue it was "patriarchy" that made him do it. But it was male-hating feminists that upset Mr. Lepine so much. So in his mind he was retaliating. Feminism made him do it.

Either way, what is wrong with both arguments is that they rely on the falseness of gender hatred, when in fact most men and women very much enjoy the opposite sex.

And "violence against women" is a myth because human violence — of which there is not a great deal in Canadian society — is a matter of wicked people of either gender who are strong, taking advantage of the weak.

In society at large it is males who commit the most violence. Of some 13,000 prisoners in Canada's federal prison system, only a few hundred are females.

But there are two things most people do not know, and should. Overwhelmingly, the victims of violent crime in Canada . . . are also males. It is for them, if for any, we should be grieving. And (are you ready?) copious research, both in Canada and the U.S., shows that females, while physically unaggressive in public, are just as violent as males in the home, where their instincts and passions are easily aroused.

Canadian researchers such as Brinkerhoff and Lupri of the

University of Calgary found the same results as American researchers Straus and Gelles, who set the standards in this field, and say that "in marked contrast to the behavior of women outside the home, women are about as violent within the family as men."

It is widely believed that wife-to-husband violence is mostly self-defence by the weaker sex. But Straus, in follow-up studies of the 428 "battered" women from his voluminous U.S. National Survey reporting the first hitter, found that husbands struck the first blow 42.6 percent of the time, and wives, 52.7 percent. Men may do more damage, body to body, but many studies show women seek weapons first, and do more serious damage with them.

For the entire last decade, 65 percent of all Canadian murder victims were males. Women tended to be killed by husbands, or live-in boyfriends, but men tended to get killed by other men — often strangers — and also by women or wives. In the U.S., about the same number of legally married wives and husbands kill each other every year — not many.

The respected American sociologist S. K. Steinmetz reports that women are 62 percent more likely than men to abuse children, that boys are twice as likely to suffer at their mothers' hands than girls, and that throughout history women have been the primary perpetrators of infanticide. And, something to ponder: the mere redefinition of the human fetus as, well, human, would convert the female sex into our largest class of murderers.

So Straus and Gelles conclude that "wife-beating" is "a political rather than a scientific term," and that violence by wives has not (yet) been defined as a problem in the public mind. This is a scientist's way of saying that on this as on so many other topics, radical feminists and left-liberals have captured the media, attempting to turn a very small problem into a huge one for political purposes.

The truth is that men and women are in this together, and we'd best stop the gender-hatred stuff and get on with a concerted effort to normalize our assumptions. Every study of violent behaviour ever done shows that the very best protection against crime is the intact traditional family, especially where there is strong religious faith, and no drug or alcohol use. Single and broken families tend to score big on sociopathology.

A classic study comparing divorce, crime, and drug-infested Nevada with the neighbouring state of Utah shows that Utah is the reverse image of Nevada on every imaginable social and health (and cost) scale. What protects Utah residents is their moral strength and determination to uphold the traditional family.

So it is not very surprising to read of a 1994 *British Medical Journal* study analysing 9,000 crimes committed in eleven different countries, showing that *two-thirds of all violent offenders and 50 percent of their victims were drunk at the time of the crime.*

Now that's sobering.

"HATE LAW" A TOMBSTONE
FOR FREE THINKING

CERTAIN ASPECTS OF the government's new "hate law" (Bill C-41) will surely serve future historians as a tombstone of sorts, marking a sharp loss of freedom and moral confusion in Canada.

Those old enough may remember large photos in *Life* magazine showing hordes of uniformed Chinese of the 1960s waving Mao's "Red Book." Brainwashed youths demanded correctness in all things, and "political re-education" of all those who had a bias or prejudice of any kind against officially promulgated views.

Secure in our superior Western freedoms, we scorned those lemming-like hordes, their minds squeezed by the steel trap of official right-think. We were horrified when students who advocated free thinking and free speech were sent before tribunals and forced to recant, or go to prison.

We are not this bad. Yet. But through a kind of gradualism, we are catching up. Most universities in Canada now have a correctness committee, and judges and tribunals here often assign "re-education" as a punishment to those foolish enough to speak their minds. Judges themselves are subjected to it by our egalitarian commissars.

Yet free societies until very recently have been distinguished from unfree ones by their reluctance to criminalize thinking. They preferred to let society punish or reward thinking and feeling through various forms of moral sanction or stigma. The formal law would almost without exception punish only actions. Hence: "sticks and stones will break my bones, but words can never hurt me."

Even today, charges of libel and slander in free nations are struck down — regardless of bias, prejudice, or hatred — if what was said is true. In short, thinking, speaking, or writing, no matter how odious to anyone else, has always been acceptable as long as it was not intended to incite violence or damage a reputation through falsehoods. It's okay to damage with truth.

But this new law specifically directs judges to find that if a crime was "motivated by bias, prejudice or hate based on the race, nationality, colour, religion, sex, age, mental or physical disability or sexual orientation of the victim" then this "shall be deemed to be aggravating circumstances." The punishment must increase.

What interests here is that the bill directs a judge to find that "bias" or "prejudice" or "hate" is always aggravating, even if a judge may feel the opposite — that a bias, say, was warranted.

Never mind the fact that, astonishingly, the bill makes no attempt to define any of these terms. It does not even allude to the difficulties that will swarm the courts of Canada over such seemingly simple words. Never mind, either, that this behaviour-based thing called "sexual orientation" cannot be defined scientifically or legally, and is repudiated by thousands of able psychiatrists. It is a political term of the times being used with great effect to secure special legal, social, economic, and now punishment rights, for what is probably Canada's most educated, and economically advantaged group.

What perceptive thinkers and writers *ought* to be screaming about is the obviously discriminatory, muzzling nature of this law, and most of all, and quite paradoxically, how the law will produce unintended consequences by favouring random violence.

Imagine, for example, two men who happen upon a crowd of journalists demonstrating in favour of free speech (don't hold your breath). Both men decide to slug two journalists in the chops. They are rightly arrested for common assault. But the judge discovers that one of them dislikes journalists because they are mostly white males. The other just enjoyed slugging someone. No motive. Bill C-41 requires the judge to give a harsher sentence to the guy with the motive, than to the one without. Random violence is better than violence with a motive.

Or imagine a religious husband who discovers his wife in a reviled act of adultery and slaps her. He will receive a harsher sentence for his action than if he just arrived home one day and slapped her for fun.

Or what if we place a person on the shore, faced with the

dilemma of jumping in to save one of two drowning people when there is no time to save both. In a flash, he will express a natural bias to save his own wife or child over another's, someone of his nation or colour over a stranger, even someone of his religion or language over an atheist or alien speaker. Such natural biases or prejudices, so expressive of bonding and community when he is good, will now be invoked for punishment when he is bad.

Parliament has blinded itself to the fact that all moral communities rely on bias and prejudice — in the healthy sense of prejudging behaviour — in order to remain communities. In fact, Canada's entire Criminal Code is itself grounded on bias and moral prejudice against thousands of behaviours that citizens and juries are expected to abhor.

From the stipulated grounds of this bill will ensue an almighty confusion, simply because human communities are centrifugal around commonly held beliefs and facts of life. Justice says that violence is violence, and a crime is a crime, but this discriminatory law does violence to that principle.

CRIMINAL INJUSTICE

IT'S A TURF WAR. Liberal criminologists (almost all criminologists), fearing a hardening of the Canadian soul, are shrieking at the public in bold headlines: "Safe to free lifers," and "Jails overcrowded," and, "Crime rate reduced." Don't believe it.

The news hasn't yet broken through our genteel national consciousness that based on the number of violent crimes per 100,000 population, the rate for Canada-the-good is up about 30 percent since the 1960s. According to the University of Ottawa's Professor Irvin Waller, director general of the International Centre for the Prevention of Crime, our rate is two or three times greater than most European countries, and nine times that of Japan.

As for the number of people in jail per 100,000 population,

the figures are: U.S., 426; Canada, 113; U.K., 97; Germany, 85; Italy, 60; Sweden, 56; Netherlands, 40; Japan, 40.

Yet even this is a strange comparison with an America which, in terms of crime, cannot be understood unless broken down into black and white subgroups, or nations — which gets criminologists into a pickle. Take murder, for example.

The U.S. rate per 100,000 is 9.3, while Canada's is 2.5. But splitting within the U.S. population produces a white U.S. rate of 5.1, and a black rate of 43.3! Against only white America we don't look quite as good. And Canada has a similar, hushed-up situation: our Native murder rate is about 25 per 100,000 (but with an insignificant effect on overall rates due to low Indian population).

With a minority status of 12 percent of the U.S. population, more than half of all U.S. prisoners are black, and Native people in both countries are way overrepresented in prisons. This is a time bomb ticking louder by the year as even liberal policymakers begin to wonder aloud how such people could be hardy enough to survive slavery, war, oppression, depression, reserves, discrimination, and poverty, then fall apart before the altruistic ministrations of the welfare state.

But regardless, we can be certain that most Canadian stakeholders in the justice system will be looking for solutions in the wrong places, based on their support of a self-serving theory of crime.

In their comprehensive book *Crime and Human Nature* (1985), Harvard professors James Q. Wilson and Richard Herrnstein argued that for the last two centuries in the Western democracies there have been two conflicting — and irreconcilable — theories of crime causation.

The hard-headed view, as I call it, was made famous by Thomas Hobbes in the seventeenth century. He described the human species as most notable for its ability to calculate personal cost-benefit decisions, and thus to seek pleasure, or avoid pain. This view says the function of punishment is "to outweigh the profit from crime." It is underpinned by the belief that our good or evil actions are decided personally.

On this theory, swift and appropriate punishment prevents greater pain to the community, and is intended not for vengeance (as critics of punishment consistently, and quite wrongly, say), but to incapacitate, to deter and, most of all, to right the moral imbalance of the community caused by crime. A debt is owed by the criminal to society.

The contrary, soft-headed view was widely promoted during the Romantic period surrounding the turn of the eighteenth century, by William Godwin and the poets Wordsworth, Blake, Shelley, and others in England — and of course by Rousseau in France. These gentlemen felt that all human beings are born naturally good, but are quickly corrupted by society and its institutions. Modern encounter-group therapies, seeking the goodness within and fired by theories of self-esteem, are based on the same beliefs. The cure for crime, they say, is not to punish criminals but to improve society so that human potential can be unleashed. Because the cause is outside us, the emphasis falls on welfare. On this view, a debt is owed by society to the criminal.

One of the main arguments we hear from supporters of the soft-headed view is that jails are ineffective, and too expensive for society.

Now, it costs about $25,000 a year to keep a U.S. prisoner

in jail, and about $48,000 for a Canadian prisoner (compared with about $8,000 for one year of parole). But before we say the economic objection is a good one, we have to ask if we have posed the right question. I think not.

The proper question would be, not "What does jail cost?" but rather, "What is the cost to society of not jailing criminals; of having them on the loose?" In short, what are the true net costs of crime?

To answer this, the Rand Corporation prepared a detailed study, *Making Confinement Decisions* (1989), to help the U.S. Justice Department analyse the net cost of crime to society. This study, based on the precise histories of 2,190 felons in four states, discovered that the average felon, while out of prison, commits an average of 187 crimes per year, at an average per-crime cost of $2,300 U.S. per felon, or $430,000 per year. (Some committed 600 felonies per year!)

If you subtract the cost of a year in jail from this total, you end up with a net cost of crime per felon, per year, of about $400,000. It costs society ten times more *not* to lock such prisoners up! The Rand study drew a lot of fire from softies for exaggerated calculations. But the need to discover the true costs of crime was established.

We need a good study on our own felons so that we can make the same reasonable calculation. We can't expect criminals to stop fooling us about their crimes, until we stop fooling ourselves about criminals.

LESS GUN CONTROL,
MORE SELF-CONTROL

Truth-seeking is pure frustration. We begin quite sure something is so, and then discover it's the opposite. The reason for this is that public life in particular is deciphered through stereotypes that haven't much to do with what's really happening. Hence, we end up with shadow policies designed for shadow problems, and the public world we think we know is what a famous critic called a "pseudo-environment."

Canada's Centre for Justice Statistics tells us that for 1991, the last full-data year, out of some 13,000 deaths from accidents, suicides, and murders combined, only five people died at the business end of a legal handgun. Meanwhile, 131 were killed with illegal handguns — and 224 by stabbing to death with the lowly knife.

So the truth is that what some call the "logic" of our national resolve to end violence by banning handguns is in fact illogical. It's a pseudo-environment, simply because illegal handguns — the ones used for the 126 remaining handgun deaths (96 percent) — cannot be banned. They are already banned. That's why they're illegal. Neither can the knife, the murder weapon of choice, be banned.

Instead of guns, what ought to be banned is our foolish and terribly costly national infatuation with a false view of what causes crime. For thirty years our academics, criminologists, and penal bureaucrats, faced with a choice between defending victims or perpetrators, have too often chosen the latter.

The normal viewpoint on crime says the human species is a calculating one. We all clearly understand the difference between good and evil (that's why even thieves don't steal when they know police are watching). Criminals differ from us not in that they don't know this distinction — but that they don't care. Retributive justice (punishment) is required, not as vengeance but to right the moral imbalance caused by each crime, and make society whole again.

In contrast, the liberal view says that we are all naturally good. Therefore evil comes from outside ourselves. It is caused by a faulty society. Fix society, and you will fix crime. Criminals should not be punished, because they are not responsible. Rather, social programs will fix society, and rehabilitation will fix the criminal.

This is a flattering, easy argument embraced mostly by the lazy-minded who have nothing to lose by being nice to criminals. And it is also profoundly opposed to common sense, and to every ethical system and religion on earth.

It was bound to have a negative result.

It did. We now have what American writer Samuel Francis describes as "anarcho-tyranny." And that's odd, indeed. After all, how can we have anarchy and tyranny at the same time?

Easy. Whole mobs of citizens taught by their culture and in the schools to express their natural desires, and who know they will not be held accountable, riot against society seeking their own form of retribution. It's a kind of soft anarchy. Instead of overthrowing society, they undermine it.

Meanwhile democratic governments, hooked on a belief system that requires the substitution of rehabilitation for punishment, soon become immobilized. Eventually, the law schools and courts become stuffed with feel-good professors and judges addicted to leniency as a form of charity and versed in twisting the law to favour criminals and tying the hands of police.

But because nothing real can be done about murder or rape ("life" means you could be out in fifteen years); or armed students assaulting teachers or each other (caning is out); about drugs, pimping, or pornography on the streets (it's just "free speech"); or about break-ins or assaults (the poor fellow was raised badly, give him a break) — governments desperately spend millions on the "optics" of crime to soothe public anxiety.

They pass draconian seat-belt laws, equip police with space-age sleuthing technology, and buy expensive photo-radar units to charge cars (not people) with crimes. They mount booze brigades at the festive season, so seven officers can openly swarm a drunk driver (while the punks swarm your store, or break into your home without a worry).

Such gelded governments also create a myriad of tribunals to regulate ideas, behaviour, and speech, to control private property, and to dictate the microdetails of business hiring, firing, paying, and pricing. It's a kind of genteel tyranny. The hope seems to be that by regulating the innocent masses perfectly, everyone will someday be perfectly good. Then there will be no criminals.

As this sort of diversionary victimization of the public increases, career criminals become freer to harm or kill again: about 60 percent of all criminals sent to our provincial and federal prisons every year have been in jail before. There are plenty of rapists and murderers who soon walk freely from Canadian jails to ply their trade again.

The name of the game, as Francis puts it, is "to avoid performing such basic functions as stopping real crime and to think up purely fictitious functions that will raise revenue, enhance the power of the police or bureaucrats, and foster the illusion that the state is doing its job."

It's not, because it can't. And that won't change until, as a people, we decide to preach less about gun control and more about self-control.

STIFLING A "SIG HEIL"

A GOOD CASE CAN BE made that inside every Canadian is a little police officer. That wouldn't be so bad, except the officer is there not to control ourselves, but others. We manage to combine ritual gentility with officiousness, and cheerfully accept a gazillion tribunals and directorates, along with quotas and correctness. Soon we'll fit Churchill's description of the wartime Germans: "They're either at your feet, or at your throat."

So when Justice Minister Allan Rock reacts to criticism of his draconian Bill C-68 gun law (that will suddenly criminalize 3,000,000 citizens if they do nothing) with "This is not an invitation for further discussion. This is final" and "We're willing to have it out right now. Let's decide who's running this country," a lot of people stifle a "Sig Heil!"

For the past three decades in particular, Canadians have been discovering that modern democracy has little to do with their consent, and rather a lot to do with the imposition of elite views by way of gutting ancient and hard-won rights and duties. On almost every issue, Canadian public policy seems contrary to the deeply held views of the people.

Although Rock won the first battle on this issue (his sizeable effort to pass Bill C-68, and to convert appearances into reality), he hasn't won the war, because an army of researchers has shown quite competently that "gun control is not crime control." That is the title of the best, must-read summary of arguments against gun control available, written by Professor Gary Mauser and published by the Fraser Institute in March 1995.

Rock has taken a sledgehammer to the fly, and has squished our freedoms in the process. And because Canadians didn't react speedily enough to reject Bill C-68, they will get far more than they bargained for. Upon passage, all Canadian firearms will effectively become the property of government because the bill says you cannot sell, dispose of, gift, or transfer a gun, even to an heir in your will. When you die it will be seized by Big Brother, without compensation. The bill allows armed, jackboot police to enter private homes and businesses any hour of day or night, on the flimsiest of pretences, to search without justifiable warrant, and confiscate without compensation. You get handcuffs, and two years in jail.

This lends an ominous credence to a *Newsweek* article that characterized right-wing worries as paranoia by citing a sentence from a militia pamphlet that warned Americans: "House-to-house searches and seizures are being conducted without warrants across the land." It should have said, Hey, look north to see this in action, folks.

But Bill C-68 goes even further, trashing many ancient freedoms and rights. Abandoning the fundamentals of our law, it criminalizes not an act, but mere possession and passivity. It denies our right to refuse cooperation with police when they break the door down, thus forcing self-incrimination. It legalizes the seizure of private property without compensation, an action we and our ancestors have been protected from for a thousand years. It creates a reverse onus by forcing the citizen to prove his innocence, rather than the state to prove his guilt. Most worrisome for all citizens, especially those in high-crime areas — it directly offends Section 7 of our Charter (our ancient right to self-defence, under "security of the person"), and Section 8 (unreasonable search and seizure).

Some critics argue that the gun control law is just another form of "interdictionism" common to elite-dominated societies: a symbolic general prohibition that provides an illusory resolution of crime. It permits the privileged, educated class that dominates the power structures of Canada to pacify the crime-bedevilled middle class. At the same time, it permits selective enforcement against the uneducated (read: uncivilized) underclass and selected ethnic targets who increasingly worry elites. History is replete with such general gun law interdictions used against: southern blacks, Italians, Reds, and, of course, against whole populations by every tyranny in history.

Most interesting will be Rock's response to Native claims to exemption on grounds that guns are a treaty right . . . when, at 3 percent of our population, Natives constitute 23 percent of all homicide suspects, and 22 percent of all victims!

The minister's four main arguments fail miserably. First, he knows there is no evidence that gun control reduces crime; it may even increase it. Second, he patronizingly worries that we may shoot ourselves (80 percent of gun deaths are suicides), yet it's Rock who wants to legalize assisted suicide as a "choice"! Third, he says we register cars, and the like, so why not guns? But cars cannot be used for self-defence, nor to protect us against intrusive governments, nor is ownership of an unregistered car (or anything else) a criminal offence.

I hope the Royal Canadian Air Farce does a skit on Rock's fourth argument, that if police "could get full details on firearms registered in [an armed household] they would be better able to plan their approach to the home."

Right. Just imagine a beat-cop calling headquarters: "It's okay, guys. Some funny sounds in there. This weird laser X on my jacket. Yeah, a little tracer smoke in the air. Some almighty poppin' noises. But honest, my good ol' Supercomputer here — thank God for good government — says there's not even a peashooter in there. Nothin'. Clean as a whistle. No need to bring rifles or reinforcements. So I guess I'll jes' step out of this here cruiser, an' take a look seeeeeee . . . "

UNJUST LAWS A DANGER TO DEMOCRACY

The PEOPLE ARE IN a fighting mood in the face of an ongoing legislative assault on their rights, community preferences, and moral values. They are told by their judges that paintings of young children engaged in sodomy and genital sucking are high art; that homosexual couples may now adopt children; that any "peace officer" or designate of the state who "believes" something, may, without a warrant, search "any place" (even a private home, using Criminal Code section 117.04(2)), with no requirement of reasonable belief that a criminal offence has been or is being committed.

In its effort to rule with the consent of the people, a sovereign parliament, especially one subject to a Charter (in other words, not so sovereign), is highly vulnerable. If wise, it will not attempt to pass any law that undermines its own legitimacy, or the law itself. For then Parliament taunts the people, and as that grand scholar A. V. Dicey warned in his 1885 tome, *The Law of the Constitution*, "the point at which subjects will offer serious or insuperable resistance to the commands of a ruler whom they generally obey, is never fixed."

But how do millions of upset citizens decide "the point," the gradation between the authority of a law and its legitimacy? After all, responsible citizens are proud to abide by any just law even if, as individuals, they disagree with it. They know we would not have a country for long if every citizen decided to obey laws selectively.

However, those who believe a law is unjust are cast at once into the dilemma of Socrates of ancient Athens, the philosopher condemned to death for corrupting youth with his teachings and who, when offered the choice to escape, refused. His grounds were that for a teacher of morals to escape a law merely because he disagrees with it casts the fundamental basis of society into disrepute.

For the ancient Greeks that made sense, because they identified good law with the good state. There could be no higher law. And this, as the great English historian Lord Acton pointed out, was "the great flaw in their vision." By equating politics with morality, they placed the supreme social-moral agent in the state, rather than above it.

Since the Middle Ages, however, the Christian notion of the enduring imperfection, even wickedness, of humans and their governments (of which we surely need no demonstration) gave birth to a revolutionary idea that later underlay the birth of democracy, and lingers powerfully still: that humans and their governments, whether monarchies or parliaments, are all subject to a higher law, descending from God, who grants rulers a conditional power.

St. Thomas Aquinas argued that even though God was the author of this higher, or natural, law (the pure concepts of freedom, love, justice, truth, etc.), it could be grasped by right reason alone. This was a revolutionary concept, as Lord Acton saw, because it gave precedence to "what ought to be" over "what is," and thus installed a "revolution in permanence." Suddenly, an individual, armed with natural law, was in a position to argue against any unjust law. Governments were horrified.

By the seventeenth century, the God part of this fell away, and political writers such as John Locke spoke not of God but of the whole people giving a conditional grant of power to government to rule by just laws. Failing this, the people always retain an inherent right to revolt simply because, when it passes unjust laws, the government makes war on the people. They have a right to self-defence. Since then, there has been one revolution after another.

Modern governments and law schools tend to discourage the use or study of natural law (though it has been a continuous force in Western civilization), invoking it — as during the Nuremberg Trials of Nazi war criminals — to punish or discipline other nations . . . but rarely themselves. The bald fact is that to the question "Why did you murder?" the Nazi generals argued, "I obeyed the law of the land." To which an international panel of judges replied: "You should have disobeyed. You knew it was unjust law." Nazis were hung for not disobeying the state.

Latent in all democracies still is the conviction that a government's grant of power flows from the people and is granted only on condition of its just use. A fair standard for the justness of a law, then, is whether it offends any basic principle of natural law or the simple foundational principles of a particular people. Such as the sanctity of private property; the right to compensation for taking property; the right to remain silent; presumption of innocence; and freedom from unreasonable search and seizure.

Justice Minister Allan Rock's gun law, Bill C-68, blatantly offends all of these rights, and more, and is widely deemed unjust by those who have suffered through a close reading. Perhaps most threatening of all, as retired RCMP Assistant Commissioner Bob Head warns, "After registration, the value of underground firearms will soar. For a hefty price, a crooked administrator could sell a list of specific gun makes, models, and addresses, and send a thief right to your home."

So there will be passive disobedience. Citizens will do nothing. They will hide weapons. Destroy certificates. Convey in secret. Buy contraband. Refuse cooperation. Remain silent. And thus our civil society will be diminished.

FALSE MERCY

IT WOULD BE NICE IF we had a capital punishment debate worthy of a vibrant people, instead of the sleepy national excuse for one that is awakened only occasionally when some public figure pulls back the sheets. Then our reflex reaction is — Quick, cover it up!

Meanwhile, the people groan to learn that about 1,100 convicted murderers are out on day parole in Canada at any one time. Some will murder again, with high certainty. Those responsible for their release will pass the buck. A Toronto man recently left his favourite restaurant in trembling disgust when he saw a new waiter approach: the man who'd murdered his daughter nineteen years before.

If ever there was an issue to sharply outline the clash between the democratic masses and their academic and media elites, it is capital punishment. The people want it. The elites do not. Generally, the people take the moral view of crime and punishment, and the elites, the therapeutic view. Elites say the only motive for killing as punishment is revenge. They generally believe that crime arises from its conditions: the perpetrator can no more be responsible for his crime than for an abscessed tooth. They say therapy — not some punishment as barbaric as the crime — is required, because the criminal is sick.

In a famous essay of 1949 criticizing this therapeutic, or humanitarian, view of justice, the British writer C. S. Lewis contrasted it neatly with the retributive view. The first sounds very nice because it appears to be mercy-based. But the hidden danger is that it dehumanizes us all by conceiving of man as a determined object, with no will of his own (otherwise he could have said no to crime, could he not?) and therefore no moral responsibility. It is thus a view which, once adopted, automatically diminishes the entire society by shunting justice to a secondary position.

He much preferred the second view that retribution — restoring the balance of justice — was fairer both to the community and to the criminal. He summarized his critique in a telling statement about just deserts (what is deserved): "The Humanitarian theory removes from punishment the concept of Desert. But the concept of Desert is the only connecting link between punishment and justice."

And for making decisions about just deserts, he felt his barber was as qualified as any therapist, who may be well qualified in theories of the subconscious, but no more so than the barber in the matter of moral justice, which is necessarily a community affair. The people are the jury.

For a century now, the therapeutic view has increasingly been used to separate punishment from justice, as if man were perfectible mechanically. But in the face of ever more barbaric crimes, it is surely time to ask a simple question: Can a society maintain civility by using a notion of individual mercy that diminishes its sense of collective justice? And never mind the merely utilitarian, and by now useless, criteria for assessing the viability of punishment: Does it incapacitate? Does it deter? Obviously, we do not incapacitate a vicious murderer by paroling him. Nor by releasing him after a euphemistic "life" sentence of fifteen, or even the maximum twenty-five, years. Neither can deterrence ever be properly measured when all punishment is delayed, lenient, and invisible to the public.

The highest and best argument for capital punishment for premeditated murder is society's need for and right to equity; for moral restoration. It is a right higher than any possible right of a murderer to enjoy the gift of life after the death of his victim. Justice should oversee mercy, not the reverse.

And importantly, the balancing satisfaction of retributive justice, even as it purges individuals of any lingering desire to kill, sends the ultimate message that killing for justice is a right of society, not of individuals. That such moral accounting must always be transferred to the larger society, where it belongs. This balancing of the books is required not because it is effective. Or a deterrent. Or because it may reform others. But simply because it is just.

Neither is it true that all deaths are equal. Any death is regrettable, but a salving, or expiatory, death does not treat a criminal "as something less than human," as the *Globe and Mail*'s Andrew Coyne put it in a recent column. Quite the contrary. It is the highest and best way for a murderer to die. It is a retributive death, a form of repayment that gives meaning back to society, as well as to the criminal's soiled life, in fact lifting him out of the animal condition to which he has consigned himself. We must consider that this, too, may be called an act of mercy. And maybe "He paid the price, fair and square" is not such a bad epitaph.

The mistaken modern liberal notion that the issue of capital punishment concerns primarily the rights of the individual criminal is deeply defective and most certainly creates a climate for heinous crime by implying that society has no transcendent claim to equity; in fact has a lesser claim against the murderer than he made against his victim.

False mercy can never produce a cohesive people, nor a truly merciful one, because it makes us accomplices in the undermining of basic justice. In time, institutionalized injustice will convert a happy national home into a motel full of frightened, disconnected egos, from sea unto sea.

V

"HEALTH" IN A SICK SOCIETY

*"Newspeak" is language designed
to make lies truthful and murder respectable.*

— GEORGE ORWELL

NO FREEDOM TO HEAL OURSELVES

I_N THE FALL OF 1995, eighty-eight stooges of the Canadian Medical Association stood up to sing the praises of state-controlled "health care" and out-vote sixty-eight of their members who boldly suggested we "should be allowed" to spend our own money on our own health, and have that right.

Boy, talk about the dark ages. Canada is still the only country in the history of the Western world to outlaw — *outlaw!* — the provision of basic private medical services.

The politicians responsible for this boondoggle saw a huge political pay-off in the imposition of universal "health" care on an unwitting and gullible population of future sickies and formerly free professionals hungry for income security.

The ostensible motive was egalitarian fairness. Tom Kent,

Prime Minister Lester Pearson's (unelected) adviser, wrote that he was "a fervent believer in medicare. I regarded it as morally wrong that money in the bank, rather than severity of need, should determine who got what health care services." Morally wrong? Okay. But because it is easy for the state to solve the money needs of the few who may lack funds, or are just too stupid or careless to buy medical insurance, only a fool or a commissar would agree with his solution. Today, it's not private money in the bank that determines who gets what, but public debt and the falling budgets of profligate governments.

So why have ordinary citizens never stood up and said: we are not forced to insure our neighbour's home, and we should not be forced to insure his body. It is wrong to ban the voluntary buying and selling of private professional services in a free society. And it's wrong to offend the Hippocratic Oath (requiring absolute confidentiality between doctor and patient) by converting by fiat the intimately private medical records of millions of citizens into potential public documents.

We have replaced rationing by price with rationing by the queue. Making you wait will either cure you or kill you. The mother of a close friend of mine died waiting for heart surgery (waiting lists are a function of budgets). Desperate, my friend had offered to pay the cost. He would borrow the money, if necessary. Operate today. "Sorry. We have an available operating room, and work-hungry nurses and doctors. But we're not allowed to accept private money from Canadians." Socialized medicine killed a Canadian mother.

An American tourist with the same sick mother? "Step right up, sir! Pleased to take your money." We take cash-paying foreigners right away. They pay double, but are not required to wait because their health care is not paid for by other Canadians. Still, many Americans come here because our medical care is cheaper even when paying cash than U.S. care. Canada's cash price for foreigners is low because it is nevertheless subsidized by Canadians. And no waiting. Last year, another friend took his closest buddy, frothing with a heart attack, to four Toronto hospitals. Turned away at each (there were available operating rooms, etc., but no staff, because no budgets), the buddy died at the fifth.

Neither have the people yet said: it is profoundly immoral to finance our "health" care (about one-third of most provincial budgets) by massive borrowing from future generations not here to defend themselves. So by now you've noticed the quotation marks around the word "health." That's because many nations — such as Italy and Japan — spend half or less per capita on what we call health care, yet are just as healthy by all standard measures. Well-regarded U.S. health economist Cotton Lindsay states that by every standard international health measure, "no [national] health plan has even a ripple of an effect on either male or female life expectancy."

So the people have not yet said: socialized medicine is obviously a political program, not a health program, that was imposed on Canadians by fiscal bribery of the provinces and legal trickery (health care is constitutionally off limits to the feds).

Nor have they said: the consequent waiting lists for services, the many thousands tripping to the U.S. for care that isn't available here, the closing of whole hospital wings despite high demand, the selective care now in place (we'll treat young, not old, this illness, but not that), the "delisting" of formerly covered services — all this results in a system that is profoundly immoral because it converts the ethic of direct Hippocratic medicine (by which formerly free physicians would do their utmost to heal all patients) into a veterinary ethic by which the quality and amount of care and resources available are now controlled by a master. A political master. We end up with the medical freedom of animals.

Neither have they said that Canada's health care system (in which the trivially ill increasingly compete by right with the truly ill) is swarming with so-called health consultants desperately trying to "rationalize" the system, who necessarily see professionals as the enemy and patients as the meat; that highly talented specialists have fled our socialized system in droves since the 1960s; that socialized medicine exerts a depressing effect on scientific research and technology; that currently the U.S., which has too many specialists, is successfully luring away legions of good GPs (my father's left Canada last year); that because Canadian political (and medical) elites are too implicated to admit the gross failure of socialized medicine, we are going to be treated to about twenty years of compensatory policy adjustments and administrative Band-Aids designed not to make us healthier, but to keep us dumb, thankful, and — most importantly — paying.

NATURE IS BAD FOR YOU

SHE SAW HERSELF AS a detective, investigating a cultural crime of great magnitude: the vast scientific deception of publics everywhere by "ideologists in a white smock" — high-level, regulatory scientists.

It's been ten years since U.S. journalist Edith Efron published her classic work of investigation, *The Apocalyptics: How Environmental Politics Controls What We Know About Cancer*. Her book was a powerful antidote to the published rants of environmental extremists who favour "lying for justice"; scaring the public with scientific fear-mongering. Rachel Carson's *Silent Spring*, Paul Ehrlich's *The Population Bomb*, were early examples.

Such books are united, she says, by a kind of visceral animosity towards capitalism, a general antitechnology attitude that characterizes modern civilization as producing "torrents of toxic and carcinogenic [cancer-causing] substances," implying that "industrial chemicals are the primary source of cancer . . . in fact the cause of 90 percent of all cancers." Most people still believe that.

Underlying this notion is the enduring flower-child conviction that nature is good, and man, "chemicals," and industry are bad. Rachel Carson wrote that "man is the only living entity that could create cancer-causing substances." Wrong. Paul Ehrlich wrote that "massive famines will occur soon, possibly in the early 1970s, certainly by the early 1980s." Wrong again.

Efron took the sharpest scalpel to all of this, and the result is liberation of the mind. She did not argue that there are no carcinogens in some industrial chemicals. But neither did she agree with such as Joseph Califano, then secretary of Health, Education and Welfare, who fulminated in 1978 that there were more than 7,000,000 industrial carcinogens. Life is just toxic hell, folks.

Shortly after his panicky outburst, however, France's IARC, one of the world's most respected cancer institutes, published a list of known industrial carcinogens. There were ten. Ten!

The difference in magnitude was astounding. Efron concluded that industrial chemical dangers have been vastly exaggerated by sloppy research, by false inferences from animal experiments (believing that if mice die of something, humans will, too), by false premises based on the "one-molecule," or "no-threshold," theory (if something in large doses is bad, then even one molecule of it is bad), and, most of all, consciously hiding the truth about natural carcinogens to keep the political heat on industry.

"Natural carcinogens"? It's mind-boggling. For natural cancers have always existed. They are even found in Egyptian mummies. Earth is bombarded daily by thousands of forms of cancerous cosmic radiation. About two dozen metals found almost everywhere in the earth's crust are carcinogenic, as is common sand dust, inhaled by us all daily. Carcinogenic asbestos is found in half of all continental bedrock. Volcanoes spew incalculable volumes of carcinogenic chemicals into the atmosphere (lead, arsenic, mercury, sulphur, and so on). Nature is bad for you!

Even ordinary oxygen is very toxic and corrosive. It is a "sink," or receptor, for the body's electrons, causes severe toxic reactions and the creation of super-oxide radicals, breaks in DNA, and in general prompts a slow poisoning. Can't live without it — or with it.

Every day lightning creates many nitrogen-based carcinogens, including ozone. Common soil worldwide is naturally radioactive, and contains most carcinogenic and mutagenic metals. Nine of the thirty-odd elements essential to life are carcinogenic. Even 100 percent pure water is highly corrosive and toxic.

As for common foods? All caffeine beverages such as teas, colas, coffees, and cocoas, and safroles in spices such as pepper, nutmeg, mace, cinnamon, and the like, and the ingredients in many fruits, dates, and strawberries, and the acetaldehydes found in all alcoholic drinks and ripe fruits — are carcinogenic. Carcinogenic plant aflatoxins, tannins, and phenols are found in food plants all over the world. Bruce Ames, a well-known

University of California professor of biochemistry and an environmentalist, recently underlined the toxicity of nature when he wrote that "99.9 percent of all pesticides that humans eat are produced by plants themselves in their own chemical defense."

Natural proteins, cholesterols, and sugars such as fructose and lactose are carcinogens. So are common salt (one billion tonnes of airborne sea salt fall on earth every year) and all forms of hydrocarbon (forests produce about 175 million tonnes of hydrocarbon every year, more than six times the amount created by man-made sources). Most cooking — smoking, barbecuing, frying, fermenting — is highly carcino-genic. Onions and garlic cooked at high temperatures are both carcinogenic and highly mutagenic. (Groan.)

This is absurd, says Efron: the very same stringent cancer standards used for the wholesale condemnation of industry, if used on the world itself, turn all of nature into a living hell.

All this doesn't mean we can't enjoy a good meal on New Year's Eve. But it does mean we have to take what scientists who lie for justice tell us with a grain of salt.

Uhhh . . . skip the salt.

CONDOMNATION

Governments, schools, and media are united in a frenzied effort to protect us all from sexual diseases. They offer a disturbing message about life's most beautiful union: Death lurks in pleasure. Whoaaoo . . .

But, holy of holies, there is salvation in latex. The condom will save you. Pleasure can be snatched from the jaws of death. Even the *Globe and Mail* will save you.

Recently the nation received its annual, and most irresponsible, editorial lecture lamenting "safe-sex fatigue," and urging a thoroughgoing use of condoms. The *Globe* had even boldly advised the nation on a prior occasion that "condoms are effective against sexually transmitted infection, including HIV."

It would seem utterly sensible to ask whether or not the latex condom will in fact do what we are told. We can certainly thank it for a degree of protection against most ordinary sexually transmitted diseases.

But the same cannot be said for the HIV virus thought to cause AIDS, which is why parents in particular should read what follows with care, and prepare to confront authorities, including schools and media — even sue them hard if their children get pregnant, sick, or die because they followed bad official advice.

I spoke to the editor of *Rubber Chemistry and Technology*, Dr. C. Michael Roland of the U.S. Naval Research Laboratory in Washington, D.C., about his research on "intrinsic flaws" in latex rubber condoms and surgical gloves (published in *Rubber World*, June 1993). The news is alarming, to say the least, and gives at least a partial answer to the *Globe*'s naive question: "Why, in spite of so much effort, does AIDS keep spreading?" Roland said that what I am about to relate is "common knowledge among good scientists who have no political agenda."

Electron microscopy reveals the HIV virus to be about 0.1 microns in size (a micron is a millionth of a metre). It is 60 times smaller than a syphilis bacterium, and 450 times smaller than a single human sperm.

The standard U.S. government leakage test (ASTM) will detect water leakage through holes only as small as 10 to 12 microns (most condoms sold in Canada are made in the U.S., but I'll mention the Canadian test below). Roland says in good tests based on these standards, 33 percent of all condoms tested allowed HIV-sized particles through, and that "spermicidal agents such as nonoxonol-9 may actually ease the passage."

Roland's paper shows electron microscopy photos of natural

latex. You can see the natural holes, or intrinsic flaws. The "inherent defects in natural rubber range between 5 and 70 microns."

And it's not as if governments don't know. A study by Dr. R. F. Carey of the U.S. Centers for Disease Control reports that "leakage of HIV-sized particles through latex condoms was detectable for as many as 29 of 89 condoms tested." These were brand new, preapproved condoms. But Roland says a closer reading of Carey's data actually yields a 78 percent HIV-leakage rate, and concludes: "That the CDC would promote condoms based on [this] study . . . suggests its agenda is concerned with something other than public health and welfare." The federal government's standard tests, he adds, "cannot detect flaws even 70 times larger than the AIDS virus." Such tests are "blind to leakage volumes less than one microliter — yet this quantity of fluid from an AIDS-infected individual has been found to contain as many as 100,000 HIV particles."

Condoms are not the solution to the tragedy of AIDS, he warns. "It is ludicrous to believe they allow one to safely engage in sexual relations with HIV carriers. Their promotion for that purpose is dangerous and irresponsible." As one U.S. surgeon memorably put it, "The HIV virus can go through a condom like a bullet through a tennis net."

It's the same story with latex gloves. Gloves from four different manufacturers revealed "pits as large as 15 microns wide and 30 microns deep." More relevant to HIV transmission, "5 micron-wide channels, penetrating the entire thickness, were found in all the gloves." He said the presence of such defects in latex "is well established."

Perhaps that is why a review of major studies shows that while condom use may reduce "rates" of infection, nevertheless the acknowledged HIV infection rate for couples using condoms is very high, ranging from 13 to 27 percent. Handing a student a condom to protect against AIDS is like giving him an overcoat to walk across a battlefield. Meanwhile, strict avoidance of sex with infected partners gives a 5,000-fold increase in protection.

For Canada, the story is the same. A standard Health and Welfare Canada test of condoms manufactured between 1987 and 1990, based on stringent tests of pressure, leakage, and volume (as in the U.S., there is no effort to examine micron-level leakage), reported that an astonishing 40 percent of the condoms tested failed at least one of the tests. Tests in 1991 showed an "improved" 28 percent rate.

On June 17, 1987, Dr. Maria Crenshaw, past president of the American Association of Sex Educators, stood up before 800 sex educators at the World Congress of Sexology, in Heidelberg, and asked a revealing question: "If you had available the partner of your dreams, and knew this person carried the HIV virus — would you rely on a condom for protection?"

There was a pregnant silence, so to speak, when not a single person raised a hand. Not one! So she accused all 800 professional sex "educators"of giving irresponsible advice to the young.

Now I'd like to know why that little scenario has never made the headlines . . .

MORE TRUTH ABOUT CONDOMS

A WISHFUL THINKER'S headline, "Condoms Can Prevent Aids," was recently plastered over letters to the *Edmonton Journal* critical of what I had written about the natural holes in latex condoms. Critics made the point that HIV tends to travel bound to a white blood cell, which is true, and therefore the natural holes in latex are "irrelevant," which is not true, because white blood cells are smaller than the largest holes in latex.

What is more disturbing, however, is the lazy and merely pragmatic logic relied on to promote condom use, heard everywhere from those suffering the moral surrender common to liberalism: the young are going to do it anyway.

So why doesn't this rule apply to everything?

For example, we know quite precisely how many young

will eventually die from smoking, alcohol, and drug use. Yet public health officials do not (yet) enter the schools handing out samples of vodka, heroin, or free cigarettes to students. In fact, they fanatically discourage smoking, drinking, and drugs — but not sex.

Imagine that the Black Death could be caught mostly by sexual contact. Would we put free condom machines in schools? I suggest not. In a mood of officious righteousness, public health officials would quarantine, or strictly control contact with, all the infected.

Instead, AIDS is the first deadly infectious disease in our history for which the infected (about 90 percent male homosexuals) are uncontrolled and roam free to infect others, while officials spend millions trying to "educate" the uninfected. To little avail. A *New England Journal of Medicine* survey reported on January 9, 1992, that "only 7 percent" of newly infected males had been warned by their homosexual partners. Infected individuals have even been allowed to give blood for public use, while timid public health officials turn their backs and glibly try to democratize the disease.

In doing so, they aid and abet sexual homicide.

On every pack of cigarettes we see a dire official WARNING about possible cancer. There are even signs in many Canadian bars — ironic, coming from an abortion-happy government — warning pregnant moms about the danger to baby from fetal alcohol syndrome. So why don't responsible health officials lobby to emboss a skull and crossbones on every condom manufactured? Then society's double message about AIDS would be fair.

"Hey, you tryin' to kill me?" would be the reaction.

Now, to the facts. There is extensive research to show that while the HIV virus may be bound to a white blood cell when carried in blood, the concern with the condom is not only blood, but infected seminal fluid, and *"tests of seminal fluid show HIV-1 to be present as free virus particles"* (V. L. Scofield, *The Journal of NIH Research*, 4, 105 [1992]). And remember: one microlitre of seminal fluid (all condom tests are blind to such small leaks) may contain 100,000 HIV particles, any one of which could pass through a normal hole in latex rubber without touching the sides.

HIV-1 particles are also found as *free particles* in pre-ejaculatory fluid (G. Ilaria et al., *The Lancet*, 340, 1469 [1992]). For parents and concerned citizens, there are many references to free HIV particles in seminal fluid in D. J. Anderson, *The Journal of NIH Research*, 4, 104 (1992).

A 1993 review of eleven published studies on condom effectiveness in reducing heterosexually transmitted HIV concluded that condoms "may only lower risk somewhat," and that "high risk behaviour" (in this case, only heterosexual intercourse with an HIV carrier) "should be . . . *eliminated"* (S. C. Weller, *Social Science and Medicine*, 36, 1635 [1993]).

As for the homosexual activity so widely normalized by media and schools? There is wide agreement among researchers that condoms afford virtually no protection during anal sex. The U.S. surgeon general has gone public on this, declaring "anal intercourse is simply too dangerous a practice."

As for condoms and other sexually transmitted diseases? More danger. The human papilloma, herpes simplex viruses, and genital warts thrive all over the external genital area, occur at a three times higher rate among teens than adults, and are all incurable. Syphilis is also at a new high. I say the happy-go-condom attitude of authorities has duped our trusting youth.

So I believe it's time to admit the so-called contraceptive model based on the condom has been a failure. The program was created in the early 1970s to reduce teen pregnancy, illegitimate birth, abortion, STDs, and promiscuity. But everywhere that it has been implemented, all these things — except for teen live births (because so many babies are being knocked off by abortion) — have skyrocketed.

By 1977, Canada's own Badgley Commission had already declared the contraceptive model of sex-ed a failure. Alan Guttmacher, formerly head of Planned Parenthood, the world's largest provider of contraceptives and abortion to school children, once agreed that the model promoted high youth promiscuity.

The U.S. Centers for Disease Control say that "50 per cent of teenagers who get abortions were using contraception at the time of conception." A Johns Hopkins study reports that 28 percent of teen pregnancies "are intentional."

Sometime soon we are going to see a study saying "50 percent of those who died of AIDS were using a condom at the time they got the virus."

But public health officials will still be sleeping quite soundly.

THE ABORTION-CANCER LINK COVERED UP

PIECE IT TOGETHER. Some 40,000 women, mostly tax-funded egalitarian radicals, descended on authoritarian China for the 1995 U.N. Conference on Women, clamouring after "reproductive rights" in the name of freedom.

What they couldn't admit is the other side of their equation. "Femicide," the widespread killing of female infants (whether in or out of the womb) because they are "the wrong sex," is considered a reproductive right and is rampant in much of the world. China registers 500,000 more boy than girl births every year. Suffocation abounds. Surprise, surprise: abortion-on-demand reinforces patriarchy. Freedom lovers cringe to hear that it was only former communist leader Mao Tse Tung's insistence on equal rights for women that temporarily halted abortion and femicide.

But there is a much more ironic spectre. Modern radicals are discovering that in her own way, Mother Nature may further trump their politics in a kind of revenge of the empty cradle: a lot of solid scientific research says women who have abortions are much more likely to die of breast cancer than if they give birth to their children.

Researchers have been stymied in efforts to explain the rapid global surge in breast-cancer rates since the 1970s. Environment, diet, age, and so on have all been factored. Yet the increase remains a mystery. But what if it's not a mystery? What if for crass political reasons it is being kept a mystery by those who stand to gain? We get the slant when Claire Hoy, author of *The Truth About Breast Cancer*, says the $7 million spent each year by the government of Ontario on four private Toronto abortion clinics is more than is spent on breast cancer research by the federal government and all provinces combined!

The fact is that millions of unsuspecting abortion clients all over the world are not being told that in 1981 the *British Journal of Cancer* published a study by Malcolm Pike showing a 2.4-fold increase (240 percent) in the risk of breast cancer for women under age thirty-three who had undergone induced abortion prior to a full-term pregnancy.

Almost fifteen years have passed, and this research, or variations of it, has been repeated in major studies in many countries of the world. In 1993, Harvard law graduate Scott Sommerville published *The Link Between Abortion and Breast Cancer*, a summary of twenty-four refereed studies in prestigious international journals showing the link. He says there is a refusal to acknowledge these studies because "feminists are more pro-abortion than anti-cancer." They worry that the whole basis for legalization of abortion in the U.S. could be reversed because the courts were persuaded that abortion is supposedly safer than a live birth.

The most recent study to land on my desk was "Risk of Breast Cancer Among Young Women: Relationship to Induced Abortion," published on November 2, 1994, in the prestigious *Journal of the National Cancer Institute.* Newspapers reported that the article said women who have abortions are at a 50 percent greater risk of breast cancer. But they did not report that it also says "induced abortion in the last month of the first trimester is associated with nearly a doubling of subsequent breast cancer risk" (a 100 percent increase), that women under eighteen who underwent induced abortion "had a subsequent 2.5-fold increase in risk" (250 percent) and if the first abortion was over age thirty, "a 2.1-fold increase in risk" (210 percent).

A Connecticut study of 3,315 mothers showed a 250 percent increase due to miscarriage (spontaneous abortion). I bet that hospitals and abortion clinics aren't handing out copies of these studies to prospective clients. And yet . . . failure to disclose readily available information on potential health risks of medical procedures is illegal. So expect a flood of suits when, if, women wake up.

The reason for the deadly connection between abortion and cancer seems to be that pregnancy initiates hormonal change promoting breast-cell growth. Once mature and specialized, breast cells are unlikely to turn cancerous. However, if this natural process is interrupted by abortion, breast cells do not complete this protective process and are far more vulnerable to cancer.

Many suspect the abortion industry has been suppressing the news, and that drug companies have been funding studies designed to repudiate the rising evidence. The favourite tactic is a charge of "recall bias," suggesting that women who get cancer are more likely to remember a prior abortion than those who don't, thus flawing studies.

Forget an abortion? Not likely. But no matter. A 1989 study by Holly Howe of the New York Department of Health, published in the highly respected *International Journal of Epidemiology*, devastated the recall-bias charge by using only women with officially recorded abortions. No fibbing possible. She found a 90 percent increased risk of breast cancer among women who had first-pregnancy abortions.

I spoke recently with a genial, somewhat doubtful, Dr. W. Hanna, research director of the Canadian Breast Cancer Foundation. But astonishingly, she had not seen any of the abovementioned studies. So I faxed them to her. I argued that with as many solid studies — even conflicting ones — on, say, the possible dangers of ozone, or cholesterol, the medical community would flash media warnings to the whole world. Why not with a possible abortion-cancer link? After all, what women need a lot more than a right to choose is a right to know.

WHEN HUMANS ARE DEFINED AS THINGS

SOMEDAY SOON, Canadians and their legislators will be put to an excruciating test of their values. Rather, they may have to face the possibility they have none at all.

Even hardened pro-abortion types (sweetly described as "pro-choice" by the media) have gagged at the new American procedure called "Dilation and Extraction." This special technique was developed for use with pregnancies as late as twenty-six weeks; that is, on sizeable, healthy babies weighing four or five pounds.

D & X is apparently not used in Canada — yet. But it is so efficient, we can be certain it will be. This clever procedure attempts to solve three problems at once. It ensures that the aborted baby cannot survive the procedure, as occasionally happens. It always kills the baby inside the mother's body, thus ensuring the physician will escape any legal charge of murdering a "born-alive" child. And finally, it allows the harvest of fresh, still-warm brain cells for medical experiments, or treatment of adult diseases.

Here's how it works, as described by American abortionist Martin Haskell, MD, who in 1992 claimed he had "performed over 700 of these procedures" and prefers it to the classic method of "dismembering the fetus inside the uterus . . . and removing the pieces." He knows a surgeon who does D & X at "up to 32 weeks or more" — that's eight months.

First, the abortionist inserts a forceps into the birth canal and starts pulling the baby out by one leg. Then, with his hands, he delivers "the torso, the shoulders, and the upper extremities," except for the head, which he intentionally leaves inside the mother. At this point, without any anaesthetic, he pushes tips of "a pair of blunt curved Metzenbaum scissors" into the back of the baby's head, and "spreads the scissors to enlarge the opening."

Next, he inserts a suction device into the hole and "evacuates the skull contents"; that is, he sucks out the baby's brains, collapsing that "skull," and pulls out the dead baby. One of the first nurses to help Haskell do this called the police. To no avail.

Inevitably, those warm brain cells will be transferred to help even the not-so-sick. An August 1992 article in the *Toronto Star* warned that future Olympic athletes may use "baby power" to win gold medals by injecting fresh fetal cells from elective abortions into injured muscle tissue. Researcher Phil Embleton said that when you are dealing with multimillion-dollar salaries, "morals go out the window." He felt the next stage would be for strength-boosting of healthy athletes.

Well, now . . . it's difficult, somehow, to thrill at the sight of a man setting a new world record in the high jump thanks to the bouncy cells of aborted babies.

But the broader political question must surely be this: How is it possible that in Canada, a "democracy" meant to reflect the will of the people, in which the majority has always disapproved of most (not all) abortions, we have no law of any kind against abortion of any kind, even those performed very late, on very large children, even — if this procedure is ever used — with the entire baby delivered, except the head?

(Significantly, the U.S. House of Representatives has voted to ban this procedure, 288 to 139. Abortionists were enraged. A *New York Times* story said, "Most of the doctors interviewed said they saw no moral difference between dismembering the fetus within the uterus [and] partially delivering it, intact, before killing it.")

A typical profile of the full range of nuanced public attitudes towards abortion — one that does not differ much between our two nations — was nicely captured in a U.S. Wirthlin Exit Poll, November 5-7, 1992. When asked "When should abortion be legal?", 4 percent said "no opinion." Only 12 percent said "at any time, for any reason." A substantial 29 percent said "only in early pregnancy." But fully 55 percent said "never, or seldom," and gave restrictive conditions, such as only to save the life of the mother, or for incest or rape.

To its credit, the liberal *Boston Globe* ran a finely detailed survey on abortion attitudes in 1989 that reflected this same picture. The survey showed that when questioned closely, even most liberals who say they support abortion on demand actually do so only in rare circumstances. The *Globe* findings strongly suggested, as another columnist put it, that even the U.S. pro-choice majority "would be ready to outlaw most of the abortions that are actually performed." So who's running these countries, anyway?

Radicals, that's who. For Canadians wondering what's in store for them, Ontario's former socialist government set the trend. Among the many mandates of then-Premier Bob Rae's "Task Force" on abortion were those actually forcing reluctant hospitals to perform abortions, and also forcing all physicians, nurses, and social workers (who continue to refuse in increasing numbers) to make "abortion referrals" regardless of personal conscience!

Alas, we have not yet figured out that the welfare state has a vested financial and managerial interest in the deliberate despiritualization of all human life, in the false concept that human beings are only material things. A $400 abortion is simply cheaper than five years of social assistance for a pregnant teenager.

Once thus conceived, our cost — and therefore our value — can be determined and weighed by the state, making us increasingly vulnerable, throughout the life cycle, to the economic manipulations of social policy experts.

Think hard about this if you or your loved one ever suffers a terminal illness in a public hospital.

Better check the orange juice.

Better yet — ask the nurse to drink a glass first.

THE STREET OF THE
DEAD FETUSES

IT HAS BEEN SAID that one death is a tragedy and a million a statistic. But on occasion a feeling person writes something so moving that a statistic is transformed into a tragedy no one understands. Irrevocably, who we are as a people changes forever through vivid moral shock.

I got the shock last week from Dr. Richard Selzer, now retired from twenty-six years as a general surgeon at Yale University Hospital. He is a compassionate man who writes from personal experience, not to lecture but to show. What he has written transcends politics. It serves as a ghastly mirror held up to liberal civilization, for we know this carefully packaged thing, in a more modernized and tidy way, happens daily in Canada . . . and it is time for all feeling people to ask why:

*

In our city, garbage is collected early in the morning. Sometimes we are resentful, mutter into our pillows, then go back to sleep. On the morning of August 6, 1975, the people of 73rd Street near Woodside Avenue do just that. When at last they rise from their beds, dress, eat breakfast and leave their houses for work . . . they close their doors and descend to the pavement.

It is midsummer. You measure the climate, decide how you feel in relation to the heat and humidity. You walk toward the bus stop. Others, your neighbours, are waiting there. It is all so familiar. All at once you step on something soft. You feel it with your foot. Even through your shoe you have the sense of something unusual, something marked by a special "give." It is a foreignness upon the pavement. Instinct pulls your foot away in an awkward little movement. You look down and see . . . a tiny naked body, its arms and legs flung apart, its head thrown back, its mouth agape, its face serious. A bird, you think, fallen from its nest. But there is no nest here on 73rd Street, no bird so big. It is rubber, then. A model, a . . . joke. Yes, that's it, a joke. And you bend to see. Because you must. And it is no joke. Such a gray softness can be but one thing. It is a baby, and dead. You cover your mouth, your eyes. You are fixed. Horror has found its chink and crawled in, and you will never be the same as you were . . .

Now you look about; another man has seen it too. Others come, people you have seen every day for years, and you hear them speak with strangely altered voices. "Look," they say, "it's a baby." There is a cry. "Here's another!" and "Another!"

and "Another!" And you follow with your gaze the index fingers of your friends pointing from the huddle where you cluster. Yes, it is true! There are more of these . . . little carcasses upon the street. And for a moment you look up to see if all the unbaptized sinless are falling from limbo.

Now the street is filling with people. There are police. They know what to do. They rope off the area, then stand guard over the enclosed space. They are controlled, methodical, these young policemen . . . Yet I do see their pallor and the sweat that breaks upon the face of one, the way another bites the lining of his cheek and holds it thus. Ambulance attendants scoop up the bodies. They scan the street; none must be overlooked. What they place upon the litter amounts to little more than a dozen pounds of human flesh. They raise the litter. And slide it home inside the ambulance, and they drive away.

You and your neighbours stand about in the street which has become for you a battlefield from which the newly slain have at last been bagged, and tagged, and dragged away. *But what shrapnel is this? By what explosion flung, these fragments that sink into the brain and fester there?* Whatever smell there is in this place becomes for you the stench of death. The people of 73rd Street do not speak to each other. It is too soon for outrage, too late for blindness. It is the time of unresisted horror.

Later, at the police station, the investigation is brisk, conclusive. It is the hospital director speaking: " . . . fetuses accidentally got mixed up with the hospital rubbish . . . were picked up by a sanitation truck. Somehow, the plastic lab bag, labeled HAZARDOUS MATERIAL, fell off the back of the truck and broke open. No, it is not known how the fetuses got in the orange plastic bag labeled HAZARDOUS MATERIAL. It is a freak accident." The hospital director wants you to know that it is not an everyday occurrence. Once in a lifetime, he says. But you have seen it, and what are his words to you now?

He grows affable, familiar, tells you that, by mistake, the fetuses got mixed up with the *other debris*. (Yes, he says other, he says debris.) He has spent the entire day trying to figure out how it happened. He wants you to know that. Somehow it matters to him. He goes on:

"Aborted fetuses that weigh one pound or less are incinerated. Those weighing over one pound are buried at the city cemetery." He says this. Now you see. It *is* orderly. It *is* sensible. The world is *not* mad. This is still a civilized society.

There is no more. You turn to leave. Outside on the street, men are talking things over, reassuring each other that the right thing is being done. But just this once, you know it isn't. You saw, and you know.

And you know, too, that the Street of the Dead Fetuses will be wherever you go. You are part of its history now, its legend. It has laid claim upon you so that you cannot entirely leave it — not ever.

Let every citizen, every teacher, ask a schoolchild to read this — and then explain what kind of people we are.

VI

A Liberal Education

*True education is what is left after you've
forgotten everything you've read.*

— AUTHOR FORGOTTEN

ONLY *PUBLIC* EDUCATION
IS IN CRISIS

THE STRANGE IDEA OF educational "reform" hit my school with a bang about forty years ago after our teacher announced with utmost gravity that "Sputnik — a small, grapefruit-sized object — has just been launched into space by the communists." A month of maths and sciences resulted.

Since then, the pattern has become clear. Education reform issues from an alternating wave-like pattern of despair and euphoria, rather like some expensive, recurring disease that eventually passes without causing too much grief. Most Canadians, echoing Mark Twain, can say: "I went to school — but I never let it interfere with my education."

For the fact is that Canada has never had a "crisis" in education. Nor is there one now. What Canada has, profoundly, is a crisis in *public* education. (Canada's 1,400 booming private schools, only about thirty of which are those elite, very good, very expensive ones, have never needed our many ministries of education with their sprawling bureaucracies to turn out fine, well-rounded graduates.)

Of course, there have always been some great public schools, too, and some great teachers in them. For the billions spent, there ought to be. But any decent reckoning will show that on the whole, government schools have failed the minds, bodies, and spirits of our children. That's because at bottom the contemporary values promoted by government schools are inherently opposed to the historical values and principles of free societies: to personal freedom (versus the public good), to the private, interdependent family (versus public services for all), to free enterprise (versus redistribution and the welfare state), and to religious faith (versus secularism, with its canon of state values).

Consider their minds. A proper economic calculation says public education is twice as expensive as the same service rendered privately. And when all costs are counted, Canada spends more per student than any other developed nation, for the worst results: costs, up 300 percent since 1960, in constant dollars. Salaries, up 50 percent. Class size, down 40 percent. A steep 30 percent drop-out rate. Twenty-five percent of Canadians illiterate (*Southam Report*, 1987). Very low scores on international tests.

As for their bodies, it's another disgrace. Lots of good North American research says bigger, fatter, weaker is the trend. We are churning out slovenly couch-potatoes, the majority of whom can't run around the block. Canadian kids have "less cardio-vascular fitness than middle-aged joggers," says University of Toronto professor Bob Goode. Even in the few public schools that do have mandatory fitness or sport classes, they're the soft, stand-around, wait-your-turn variety. Most private schools, in contrast, incorporate serious sport into their philosophy of training the whole person.

As for their spirits and values? Public schools in particular, and many of the textbooks they use, are deeply, if mostly implicitly, anti-God, anti-tradition, pro-government, anti-free-enterprise, and yes, implicitly, often explicitly, anti-family. Always, the family is presented as the competition for the allegiance of the student to more statist values.

This tradition goes back to Plato, and more recently to the Marquis de Sade, who in 1789 said the family child was owned by the French state. In 1978, his alter ego, our own Laurier LaPierre, spoke against the family on behalf of yet another educational commission when he announced that "the child is not a family child. He is an institutional child. It is not the school that is the extension of the home, but the home that is the extension of the school." In 1991, Calgary's former board of education chairman Alex Proudfoot echoed this same belief when he told a group of astonished parents, "The child is not your child, [children] are property of the state, like our oil . . ."

Canadians haven't yet figured out that any educational organization must inevitably serve as a trustee of the child for someone. Generally, for the master who delivers the pay cheque. That's the government, for public schools; the parents and their community, for private schools. But it cannot serve both with integrity.

As bureaucracies eat up an increasingly large percentage of dollars ostensibly extracted for "education," the public discovers that the number of teachers as a percentage of the adults employed by the whole education system keeps going down, and the product continues to decline. More retooling is therefore announced to offset a new public despair cycle and create a new euphoria. For this, there has been a witch's brew of magical solutions, many of which linger in some crippled form: Progressive Education (thanks to Rousseau, and John Dewey); Enriched Education; Mastery Learning; Whole Language; the New Math; Open Classrooms; Activity Groups; Ungraded Schools; Magnet Schools; Academy Schools; Developmentally Appropriate Practices; Computer Education; Outcome-Based Education; Charter Schools; and so on.

But this is mere marketing jazz. Government cannot solve the problems of public education, because government is itself the problem, and no amount of tinkering, or inviting "dialogue" or "input" from parents will change anything unless the paymaster is changed. Parents must insist on the right to pay their school directly, withdraw support, or give their funds to a better school if they see fit. The appropriate values, principles, and standards will quickly follow.

VOUCHING FOR
THE VOUCHER SYSTEM

To JUDGE FROM THE avalanche
of letters-to-the-editor my writings have sparked, critics of
my views on the dangers of public education have suffered far
too much of it.

What we get is the same old spectacle of entrenched vested
interests arguing insanely to protect their turf by ignoring the
educational trinity of mind, body, and spirit. But as I said, the
game is over: on the whole, in the long run, despite even the
best intentions, public education cannot be successful
because it is run by government, and inherent in all government enterprise is a tendency both to crowd out the resources
intended for the consumers of the service and to displace
community values with state values.

What's needed to reverse this is structural change to ensure that the party with the greatest interest in the educational trinity always has the option to directly reward or punish the service provider.

Who is that party? The parents.

Parents need choice in education.

While not perfect, some form of voucher system would at least begin the process by changing the paymaster from government to parents. All parents should receive one educational voucher worth the per-capita unit cost of education for each child, and be allowed to spend it at any school of their choice. No government needed. Gone.

The parents will be the first to discover bad schools, and the first to find a better. Overnight, public schools would get what they fear most: competition for quality, discipline, and standards, all stemming from competition for parental approval — and dollars. Bad teachers hate such competition. Good teachers welcome it. To test the idea, just answer this question: If we had such a system, and the government tried to compete, would you give your voucher to a private school or a government school? I wager even most public-school teachers would send their own kids to private schools. Many already do.

And sky-high drop-out rates and illiteracy rates would soon tumble. Contrary to the charge of exaggeration from my critics, these can't get much worse. Statistics Canada's 1990 literacy report for the National Literacy Secretariat (which "builds upon" a 1987 Southam survey) merely chops up the bad news. It divides numeracy and reading skills into three or four levels that range from low (barely "recognizes" a number, or "cannot read"), to high ("enables them to meet most everyday demands"). That's "most" everyday demands. Not all demands. Even Statscan's highest literacy/numeracy level aims low. Examples of everyday demands at the highest level were: calculating a simple bank deposit slip, figuring out a swimming pool schedule, or writing a letter to complain about an appliance. None of this is about true literacy, but only about getting by.

Actually, Statistics Canada tells a story that glides over an appalling situation. First, its target survey group is neither representative nor random. Residents of the Yukon and North West Territories, of the armed forces, those on Indian reserves, and inmates of institutions were not included in the sample. Thousands of Canadians known to have the very lowest abilities were intentionally left out. Second, the analysis and descriptive language are everywhere too flattering: even having no skill is called a skill.

And I was dead wrong on the 25 percent illiteracy figure that critics say I've exaggerated. It is much higher! According to Statscan, it's actually 38 percent for numeracy when you add up those who were stopped by level 1 (24 percent) and level 2 (an "additional" 14 percent). And I'm not including the "estimated 820,000" who were excluded because they couldn't read either official language of Canada, or couldn't understand the most basic questions. An additional whopping 1.2 million Canadians apparently undertook, but "refused to complete," the writing tasks. If because they were unable, this reality ought to have been included.

But here's the rub for teachers: a measly 64 percent of those who actually completed high school reached the highest (and very undemanding) numeracy level. In other words, 36 percent of all of our graduates are not sure to get through the every-day, number wise. So my question is, How did they graduate? Even worse: of those sixteen to twenty-four years of age (prime student years), fully 44 percent didn't get past level 2!

It's time to ask for our money back.

As for reading? More bad news. Not my 25 percent, but again fully 38 percent of Canadians cannot reach the highest everyday level. And fully 47 percent of Canadians could not write a simple letter requesting the repair of an appliance.

Here's more: only 70 percent of those "with high school completion" make it to level 4. Public-school teachers are grad-uating a lot of ignoramuses, and devaluing the high-school degree in the process. It's a rip-off.

Never mind the public-university scam: fully 7 percent of those "with a bachelor's degree or above," and 16 percent of those with a community-college diploma or certificate, could not make level 4. As supposedly educated people go, they're illiterate — with a degree to prove it.

So there's the picture: stupefying illiteracy rates; shameful drop-out rates (even if we accept Statscan's padded number of 18 to 20 percent, it's very bad. Germany's rate is 10 percent; Japan's, 2 percent); and unconscionably high per-capita costs.

It's time for parents to assume the direct responsibility they ought never to have surrendered, and take back their schools.

THE EDUCATIONAL
JACKBOOT

THE ONE THING THEY will not recommend, these high-paid gurus on our public education commissions, is what true education requires if it is to be called education.

They will mention the "need" for more teacher training, early education, social services, a new-fangled community council, or "input" to the educational sausage-grinder from those breeding-machines called parents.

They will produce multimillion-dollar studies directed by rusty old lefties like Ontario's Gerald Caplan and (My Gawd — she's still at it!) Monique Bégin, the Trudeau-Lalonde federal stalwart who engineered the budget-busting tax extortion and transfer-payment bribery behind Canada's "free" health care.

Okay. We get it now. It's the sound of the Great Canadian

Syllogism: everything must be done by government. Everything is a failure. Therefore everything will be fixed by government. Bang: hard head of bull hits brick wall.

The public-education problem is what mathematicians call a "strange loop." Example: the sentence, "It is true that everything I say is false," is a self-referential, self-contradictory loop. We get trapped by its weird logic. By the same token, highly paid government educators are hopelessly trapped in the strange loop called education. They refuse to say the only thing that will disentangle: That true education is simply about the development of wisdom, character, and leadership, and no system of government education can reliably produce these things. Some kids are headed for excellence, regardless. They will manage to escape the damping effects of the system. But for the rest — most — public education can be expected reliably to aim for and produce the opposite.

The reason is that to learn well and be wise, of high character, a leader, means not to be like everyone else. It means to be different, it means (here comes the "B" word, and the sound of many egalitarians choking) to be better. To be what we all want our children to be. And that's undemocratic, in the modern sense.

Half a century ago, the very wise and learned Harvard professor Irving Babbitt put this dilemma thus: "The democratic contention that everybody should have a chance is excellent, provided it means that everybody is to have a chance to measure up to high standards. If the democratic extension of opportunity is, on the other hand, made a pretext for lowering standards, democracy is, insofar, incompatible with civilization."

Now here's the rub. In the early days, before the government education machine really got gyrating, the system worked modestly well. Public educators then, as now, saw it as their task in life to shape in a common mould the little souls entrusted to them. To put old heads on young bodies. Public servants took oaths swearing to uphold religious and community-parental values. All agreed to teach the things for which 115,000 Canadians have died in Canada's wars (but which are mostly off the public-education table today): liberty, piety, humility, family, free enterprise, self-reliance, high character, and a deep repugnance for government interference with these things.

It was always understood that very few would ever be true leaders — mass leadership being a contradiction in terms. Educators were aware, as Babbitt again put it, "that true liberty requires a hierarchy and a subordination," most of all to some ethical centre, some set of values with reference to which both individuals and governments must control themselves. Self-control was the highest aim both of private character and public institutions. Both America's and Canada's constitutional democracies were designed with this control factor — checks and balances — deeply in mind.

But modern egalitarian educators are hooked on the opposite, Jeffersonian assumption (he inhaled it from the revolutionist Rousseau) that all humans are naturally good. This, Babbitt described as "the most centrifugal doctrine the world has ever known — the doctrine that encourages men to put their rights before their duties."

Modern education is therefore no longer rooted in an ethics, the conviction that for unformed children there is a constellation of ennobling values and standards to be learned at some pain from exemplary teachers, but in a flawed psychology. In the idea not of self-control, but self-release (to let that goodie-goodness out). It is about self-esteem (rather than earning esteem from others for one's estimable behaviour). About creating one's very own value system (a common standard of morality is said to be oppressive, or "judgemental"). About deserving equality of social and economic outcomes (regardless of personal talent or effort, because the idea of excellence, leadership, and — oh dear — competition . . . is really only "socio-economic class bias"). It is about rights without effort or duties.

The political result in government schools is that the original notion of democracy, the first system in history intended to get the masses free — not from a common ethics, but from the political jackboot — to permit the fullest, freest development of inherently unequal human talents, has been perverted into a stifling egalitarian ideal served up as educational Pablum to stop up the mouths of our children.

The jackboot is in the classroom, and the door is closed.

JUNK SCIENCE

WHY DO TEACHERS SO often force-feed kids one-sided facts and theories about the world? Wouldn't education be much more stimulating if schools focused on broad underlying debates instead of on assumed dogma?

For example, over the years my children have all heard scary lectures on "global warming." They learn that global temperatures could rise 5 to 10 degrees celsius in the next fifty years mostly because of burning fossil fuels. Polar ice-caps could melt. Oceans might flood coastal cities.

No wonder kids want to be tucked in at night!

A thorough teacher would have told them this was just one dismal theory; there is no convincing scientific proof of global warming. In a 1993 poll of U.S. meteorologists, 49 percent said there has been no global warming, 33 percent said "don't know," and only 18 percent thought there had been some. While we have more carbon dioxide in the atmosphere than a few decades ago, we had tonnes more a few million years ago — and maybe could use a lot more: global warming would be a boon to food production worldwide.

This teacher could also add that any global warming may only be part of a huge natural cycle (trees once grew near both North and South poles); that we have just finished a mini ice age; that a melting north polar ice-cap won't flood anything because when ice floating in water melts, the water does not rise — Archimedes Law (and even a global rise of 10 degrees will only raise polar averages to -40C). That when Mount Pinatubo blew up, it spewed more greenhouse gas into the atmosphere than all human activity since the Industrial Revolution. And anyway, natural fluctuations of carbon dioxide absorption in the oceans and biomass dwarf anything humans produce. Of high interest, too, is that "global cooling" theory predicting a new ice age may be on the comeback because warming (if true) could create more snow and ice at the poles, locking up more of the earth's moisture, and . . . lowering the oceans.

Now, children, let's discuss all this . . .

It's the same with acid rain. Sure, it exists. Class notes give the standard equations for conversion of greenhouse gas into acid rain. Okay. But that doesn't explain why coring samples of 800-year-old sediments (long before the industrial age) from freshwater lakes in Scandinavia, Nova Scotia, and the Adirondacks of the northeastern U.S. show acidity levels higher than today. Or why, as Illinois soil scientist Edward C.

Krug put it, "the magnitude of acidic surface waters in areas without acid rain dwarfs that of areas supposedly 'devastated' by acid rain." But I bet your kids won't hear this.

Overpopulation is another dogma in the schools. Children can be relied on to inform their parents, with teacher-induced pugnacious confidence, that the world has "too many people." They should ask their teachers G. K. Chesterton's question: "If the world has a surplus population — are you part of the surplus? And if not, how do you know?" They're not told that no one has a clue on future population: in 1992 the U.N. Population Division forecasted a world population for the year 2150 ranging from 27 billion down to 4 billion — less than today. More worrisome, your kids are not told that Canadians, and the people of most other democracies, are not reproducing themselves, so we can expect a massive die-off and birth-dearth.

Also, density creates wealth. The most densely populated countries and cities on average tend to be the most wealthy. Although zany U.S. catastrophist Paul Ehrlich predicted in 1965 that 60,000,000 Americans would die of starvation by the year 2000, in fact world food production has outstripped population growth ever since 1977. And imagine this: allowing a coffin-sized space for each person, the entire five-billion-plus people on earth could be stuffed into a single box just over a mile square and shoved over the Grand Canyon — and you'd still look down on it! It's a surprise to learn that only about 1 percent of the earth's land surface is actually used for human habitation.

And then there is Darwin. Children are regularly told to learn Darwin's 1859 theory of evolution (you know: from non-life, to cell, to invertebrate, to fish, to amphibian, to reptile, to mammal, to primate, to man) as a scientific fact, instead of as a mere theory, which is what Darwin knew it was. He was certain that completion of the fossil record would eventually show a regular evolutionary gradation, instead of separate species with huge gaps between them. But — surprise — no true, undisputed transitional types have been found. All animal and plant species appeared suddenly in the fossil record, and are as separate as ever. Species do not change into other species. Even Harvard's Stephen Jay Gould, an evolutionist, says the highly embarrassing rarity of transitional forms is "the trade secret of paleontology."

The really exciting educational fact here is that Darwin's theory of evolution has been attacked with increasing severity and power this century by prestigious paleontologists, geologists, transformed cladists, discontinuists, molecular biologists, creationists (religious as well as atheistic), and proponents of intelligent design. How exciting. Here is a field that shook the world, getting shaken down itself. A theory that shook religion . . . has become a religion!

But you wouldn't know it to read most school textbooks or class notes. There you find more interest in confining students to stale theories, junk science, and politicized social theory than offering the far more interesting and complicated truth. Too bad.

DARWIN'S MONKEY BUSINESS

Pssst! Don't tell. The most explosive secret of the worldwide intellectual establishment is the rapid crumbling of Darwinian evolution theory. At the 1966 Wistar Institute Symposium, Sir Peter Medawar expressed this widespread skepticism on behalf of an imposing assembly of scientists. The fantastical idea that all life began from non-life, then evolved by gradual random mutation and natural selection from a single-celled common ancestor into complex higher life forms, has fallen on hard times.

Molecular biologist Michael Denton spoke for many doubters in his lucid *Evolution: A Theory in Crisis* when he wrote that "ultimately the Darwinian theory of evolution is . . . the great cosmogenic myth of the twentieth century." It's a pseudo-scientific Genesis story that presents God as a natural blind process instead of as a purposeful creator. Well, the reputational fur — uh, feathers — are flying.

And yet the broader public is largely unaware of this bitter dispute. Museums and textbooks continue to display standard models of, for example, the famous "horse sequence" (tiny weird horse transforms into normal big horse over millennia). But Dr. Niles Eldredge, a curator of the American Museum of Natural History, says "[the horse sequence] has been presented as the literal truth in textbook after textbook" and complains that this is both "speculative" and "lamentable." Meaning, possibly, a lie.

The public also believes all critics of evolution theory are religious nuts, when in fact the main thrust of criticism comes from a wide variety of fields within science itself, mostly from agnostics doubting Darwin as much as God.

Their main bone (sorry) of contention is that if Darwin's theory of random mutation and natural selection were true, then just as there is plenty of fossil evidence for all the known species, there ought to be lots of it for the millions of "transitional forms" of plants and animals that gradually evolved into their final forms.

But no siree. Once a loon, or a bat, or a lobster, well, that's it. You're stuck. For 500,000,000 years, from first lobster fossil to the living model dropped in your boiling kettle — there's no change. The overwhelming impression to be gotten from a study of the fossil record is not evolution, but stasis. No one has ever found a maybe, or partly loon, or bat, or horse. You know, something on the way to becoming those species from whatever they were before.

Some argue that even the basic idea of gradual evolution is

self-defeating because if species depend on optimal adaptation for survival, then anything on the way to becoming optimal couldn't survive to adapt, could it?

And then there's the problem of simultaneity. The evolution of interactive parts of organisms (the iris, the cornea, the eyelid flap, say) would all have to change at once. How could a blind process orchestrate such harmony?

There is no good answer. And that's why Darwin himself said "the [human] eye, to this day, gives me a cold shudder," and, "the sight of a feather in a peacock's tail . . . makes me sick."

Perhaps the most disturbing fact for evolutionists is that more than three-quarters of the earth's crust is lifeless. No fossils. Then, in the so-called Cambrian explosion, life suddenly appears, demonstrating most of the same species we know today, with the same huge gaps between them, and no evidence of any transitional forms whatsoever. Even modern agnostic scientists routinely refer to this as "abrupt appearance," or "creation."

Fish appeared abruptly in complex form (Ommanney: "a veritable explosion"); same with reptiles, and birds (Ager: "we find not gradual evolution, but . . . sudden explosion"); and the primates, says Johansen, "spring out of nowhere, as it were. They are here today. They have no yesterday."

It's the same for man. Geneticist Richard C. Lewontin, former president of the Society for the Study of Evolution, and professor of zoology at Harvard, says, "There is a vast weight of empirical evidence about the universe which says that unless you invoke supernatural causes, the birds [life in general] could not have arisen from muck by any natural processes" (though he prefers a natural answer). And about man evolving from apes, he says in his 1982 book, *Human Diversity*, "All the fossils which have been dug up and are claimed to be ancestors — we haven't the faintest idea whether they are ancestors."

Probability crunchers, information theorists, and molecular biologists are also weighing in against evolution theory. Computers programmed to mimic Darwinian evolution just jam up. The likelihood of random creation of only one single protein (of some 200,000 human proteins) is one in one billion. So Nobel laureate Francis Crick, discoverer of DNA, says the whole field has "too much speculation running after too few facts" and has suggested life came to earth by "panspermia" — seeding from outer space. According to the famous astronomer and mathematics professor Fred Hoyle, the information content of a single enzyme is unimaginably vast. "Evolutionary processes would require several Hubble times [the time since creation of the universe]. The chance that higher life forms might have emerged in this way is comparable with the chance that a tornado sweeping through a junk-yard might assemble a Boeing 747 from the materials therein."

By now, Darwin's theory sounds like monkey business.

CANADA'S SLAVE TRADITION

SLAVERY? IN CANADA? HOW
could it be? A little booklet called *Slavery and Freedom in
Niagara*, by authors Michael Power and Nancy Butler of
Welland, Ontario, recently landed on my desk and got me
going on this subject. In school we learn only that Canada-
the-good served as a kind of Holy Land for persecuted slaves
who escaped from a barbaric U.S. This has created an unjusti-
fied belief in our moral superiority, and our schools should set
our children straight.

For around the year 1780 there were an estimated 4,000
blacks living in the Canadian British colonies, of whom about
1,800 were slaves. Canada's first antislavery law (of sorts), of
July 9, 1793, did not exactly outlaw slavery. It was called "An
Act to Prevent the Future Introduction of Slaves." In other

words, slavery would remain legal, but no more slaves could be imported to Canada.

Now it is easy to spring to judgement on all this, until we recall that slavery, practised at some point prior to this century by almost every known civilization, and defended by Plato and Aristotle as "natural," was until very recently protected by international law. In the eighteenth century, even freedom philosopher John Locke argued that being a slave to the victor was morally preferable to dying as a prisoner of war.

Slavery was widely practised in Africa for millennia by blacks who sold blacks to each other, to Arabs, and to whites. The U.S. census of 1830 records that 10,000 slaves were owned by "free men of colour." The last nations to outlaw slavery were those on the Arab peninsula, in 1962. There is evidence that slavery is still practised in the Sudan today.

When Columbus arrived in the New World in 1492, he discovered that slavery, along with cannibalism and torture, was already widely practised by the local Tiano, Arawak, and Carib tribes. Many American and Canadian Indian tribes, such as the Tonkawa of Texas, or the Kwakiutl of British Columbia, had been slaveholders (or cannibals, or both) since forever. At the time of white conquest, up to 15 percent of the Kwakiutl were slaves to their own powerful chiefs. White Europeans arrived in Mexico horrified to discover an Aztec civilization built on slavery, human sacrifice, and cannibalism of up to 250,000 slaves per year!

As for pioneer Canada, Power and Butler write that "slave owning was widespread among the emerging political and social elites of Upper Canada." Peter Russell, Matthew Elliot, and many other distinguished men who sat on the Legislative Council of Upper Canada each owned dozens of slaves.

Most sought to protect their "right" to own slaves by arguing that a slave was legally owned property, and the right to own property was basic to all free societies. Courts that took away legally owned slaves could also take away land, or homes, and then tyranny would reign.

Farmers asked, Who will compensate us for our freed slaves, and the lost benefits from slave labour? Many settlers were Loyalists who came here because government had promised them cheap land on the condition that they clear it. So slaves were purchased specifically for that purpose. The government had lured them. Was the government now going to ruin them?

An irony of the history of slavery in Canada is that many individual U.S. states (Delaware, Michigan, Rhode Island, and Connecticut) had banned slavery outright twenty years before Canada prohibited (only) the future importation of slaves. So the state of Michigan, Power and Butler write, became "an instant haven for slaves escaping from Upper Canada"! Canadian slave owners complained bitterly, imploring our Lieutenant-Governor to stop what was in effect a reverse underground railroad. He refused.

A friend of mine, expressing his instant moral repugnance, asked, "How could they not see the immorality of it?" I replied, "Just like we do not see our own." Slaves were legally defined as non-persons. Might future moralists not wonder, for example, at our own tortuous moral and legal chicanery granting modern mothers the legal "right" to vacuum out — or even crush heads and tear limbs off — babies in their own wombs? They can do so only because the unborn human baby is defined in our criminal law as a "fetus," a non-person. The very same modern liberals who violently deplore slavery, violently defend the right to abortion on demand. They don't "see" their immorality.

Are we much better off? In past times, though less than 5 percent in North America were slaves, the average citizen, white or black, was quite free of the thousands of meddling laws and controls that deeply invade our privacy — and had to pay not a penny of income tax. Yet today entire populations in the "free world" are tax slaves to massive governments for more than half of every year of their lives — and face physical imprisonment if they refuse to pay. Ownership is not necessary. That's why the American revolutionist Josiah Quincy cried out against tax slavery in 1774, saying, "I speak it with grief — I speak it with anguish — I speak it with shame — I speak it with indignation — we are slaves, the most abject sort of slaves."

DEFIANT TOWNFOLK
DEFEND A SLAVE

H<small>E COULD HARDLY</small> believe his ears when his master said, "Take my best horse, Solomon, and deliver this message to our good neighbour." He had been entrusted with a high duty.

Thus began the little-known story of Solomon Moseby (for which thanks are owed to Welland, Ontario, historians Michael Power and Nancy Butler, authors of *Slavery and Freedom in Niagara*, and to eyewitnesses who recorded this in 1897).

For as his heart quickened with the pace of the horse, as he rode in perfect harmony with the sunlit streams and the fresh smells of spring, Solomon dared to wonder what freedom might be like.

Irresistibly, he headed straight north to Fort Niagara (now Niagara-on-the-Lake; then, the capital of Upper Canada and

having 400 black residents, a tenth of the town's population).
After two arduous months Moseby arrived, wept with joy —
and received a terrible shock. Incensed at the theft of a fine
horse, his master had tracked Moseby all the way. He complained bitterly to the Lieutenant-Governor of Upper Canada,
Sir Francis Bond Head, who jailed Moseby as a thief.

The people were outraged. Wasn't this a hero escaping bitter
torment? Citizens, white and black, signed a petition cleverly
arguing that because a slave was property, and not a person,
he was not a free agent and therefore could not be morally or
legally guilty of a crime.

Bond Head deliberated deeply on this point, and ruled
against them. "This land of liberty," he declared, "cannot be
made an asylum for the guilty of any colour."

Now here was a whole town of angry citizens claiming
high moral principle to free Moseby — while their leader
declared a higher one to jail him. It was moral gridlock.

The next day, something magical happened. The local
preacher, Hubert Holmes, upon hearing Moseby was to be
returned to slavery, thundered, "Never while I live!"

Black runners (risking capture by "black ruffians, as well as
white," who made a living returning escaped slaves to the
Americans for money) were sent off each chilly night to get
recruits. Blacks everywhere dropped their tools and headed
for Niagara. The people bristled with anger, the towns were in
ferment.

Temporary shacks, at first a dozen, then hundreds, sprang
up around the jail. Captain Richardson of the ferry "Canada"
rebuffed Bond Head, swearing "no vessel commanded by me
will be used to convey a man back to slavery!"

One week went by. No toilets. No food or water. Cold nights without blankets. The black brotherhood watched, and sang. And hundreds of the white townfolk fed them, gave blankets, and took many into their homes.

Sir Bond Head said they will grow tired. They will be hungry. They will go home. But after three weeks, there was a siege shantytown of some 400 blacks on public grounds. Their campfires burned to sweet singing voices.

On the last day, the prisoner was dragged out between armed constables to a wagon pulled by two fiery horses. Soldiers with fixed bayonets fended off the angry crowd. The rooftops were covered with whites and blacks shouting to stop this horrible deed, as the terrified, handcuffed Moseby was pushed into the wagon. Then, just as the Riot Act against insurrection was read, and the crowd grew angrier with each word, "the gates were thrown open, and the spirited team came out with a rush."

Frightened horses reared. Women threw rocks at the guards. Sheriff McLeod "went up and down, slashing with his sword . . . and many of our people had cuts on their necks."

Boldly, Preacher Holmes grabbed the reins, while Jacob Green shoved a fence rail through the spokes of the wheels. A confused Sheriff McLeod on his stamping horse was blocked by a large black woman, who would not move aside, "her ponderosity happily offering an effectual bar, but on whom he hesitated to use his sword."

Seeing the horses stopped dead, and fearing mayhem, he shouted "Fire!" So one soldier shot preacher Holmes straight through the heart. Another ran his bayonet through Green as he struggled to get away.

Amidst the furor, Moseby leaped out of the wagon and disappeared into the night. One witness said the jail guard intentionally hadn't locked the cuffs; another, that the blacksmith had made them to open easily.

Forty blacks were jailed for insurrection. At the trial, the death of Holmes was declared "justifiable homicide." But for months to come, Upper Canada's newspapers continued the debate. One paper said Moseby was a hero; another, an ungrateful villain provoking civil disorder.

But by December 4 the Mackenzie Rebellion was under way, so the prisoners were released to fight for Canada in a special black platoon. Meanwhile, having heard of their jail plight, an American force had moved close to Niagara to "liberate" the blacks from British Rule in the name of "republican democracy."

But wanting none of that sort of "freedom," our black soldiers begged permission to fight them and thus "to defend the glorious institutions of Great Britain."

While all this unfolded, Moseby somehow got to England, where he became legally freed. Years later, he returned to a Niagara somewhat reluctant to forgive him the sadness provoked in their midst.

It's time for the CBC to make this great Canadian story an equally great documentary.

VII

THE MORALITY THING

Moral goodness is the child of habit.

— *ARISTOTLE (384-322 B.C.)*, NICOMACHEAN ETHICS

SPECTRES OF
"REASON"

IN ONE OF THOSE unctuous
political utterances for which he is notorious, British prime
minister John Major declared that "fascism and communism
lie behind us. The two great enemies of reason have been
defeated." Astonishing, coming from a nation that spent so
much blood fighting these evils — and dead wrong on three
counts.

First, fascism and communism may be napping, but they
are not comatose. Their roots are far too deep for that. Several
Eastern European nations, after having been joyously liberated
from the horrors of communism in the '90s, turned right
around and freely voted it back into power with only a slight
change of make-up. As for the much misunderstood fascism,
there are signs of it everywhere, both in Europe and in North

America, especially in the schools and universities, which heavily promote ethnic identitarianism.

Second, the implication of his comment was that communism is a demented expression of the left, and fascism, of the right. As a good pluralist, Major wished to blame them equally. Leftist journalists and undergraduates are always eager to echo this balancing reflex by quickly labelling anyone with non-egalitarian views a "fascist."

But third, fascism and communism were in fact both revolutionary, if rival, brands of socialism. Fascism sought to build socialism on national unity (most notably in Italy and Germany), while communism sought — still seeks — to transcend the level of the nation by building socialism internationally. Desperate to distance themselves from Hitlerism, the internationalists simply persuaded compliant intellectuals to label his fascist socialism "right wing."

But no form of socialism can ever be conservative, except in the perverse and ironic sense that it seeks to permanently rigidify and freeze society in an unchanging utopian mould by suppressing human freedoms and the differences that naturally arise in free societies.

As commonly understood, however, neither of these sibling ideologies was "conservative." For neither sought to preserve the enduring moral and civil values of a free society against the plundering state. Quite the reverse. Although they used the title of "democracy" and claimed to fulfil the will of the people, each worshipped a strong, totalitarian state, and was deeply opposed to capitalism.

They also scorned private property, ridiculed our central belief in individual liberty as the basis of civilization, and were profoundly atheistic, placing great stock instead in the mystical appeal of statism. Mussolini was positively rhapsodic in his claims that fascism reasserts the rights of the state and "its ethical will," which expresses "the real essence of the individual." And each produced dictators with absolute, god-like control over their own people. In brief, both were proudly collectivist, antheap ideologies. Always will be.

Most interesting, however, is the charge they were "enemies of reason." For if fascism and communism (or socialism in any of its forms) are anything, they are the highest expression of naked "reason," if by reason we mean the logical unfolding of a single political theory, unchecked by liberty and religious or moral norms.

And that is the Western disease. Marx's *Das Kapital* is a tortuously "reasoned" book. Infuriatingly so. That is its great appeal to deracinated Western intellectuals. It literally marches from one persuasive (but false) assumption to the next, and, unbeknownst to admirers in its spell, leads like iron rails not to utopia but to the concentration camps. Hitler's *Mein Kampf* is the same. Tightly, and falsely, reasoned. Mussolini's essays were beauties of reason — if you love statism.

The roots of all this are deep, and burst upon the world for the first time in the intensely reasoned democratic theories of the French Revolution. The revolutionaries hastened to "dechristianize" France (because religion was deemed so irrational) by dragging crucifixes through the streets, smashing churches, and guillotining priests. Whereupon Notre Dame Cathedral was renamed the "Temple of Reason." Inside, a gimcrack Greco-Roman structure was built of linen and papier mâché, and a toga-clad opera singer playing the part of

Liberty sang and bowed to the flame of Reason. In the cathedral of Saint-Jean, a "Feast of Reason" was held, where supplicants sang anti-hymns celebrating "Reason as the Supreme Being."

At the start of the Second World War, Hitler proudly chortled, "This revolution of ours [National Socialism] is the exact counterpart of the French Revolution."

British philosopher Michael Oakeshott concluded of fascism, communism, and national socialism: "The doctrine of representative democracy . . . is the parent of these ungracious children."

And G. K. Chesterton noted that a crazy person is one "who has lost everything except his reason." That is, has lost moral norms and standards of decency — but not brute logic. Reason without moral and social norms leads to disaster.

It's the same for nations. As another wise observer put it, neither fascism nor communism was a relapse into the dark ages, nor a flight from reason, but rather, the "fulfilment" of reason.

NEW RIGHT TALKS
LIKE OLD LEFT

To THE QUESTION "Who are we, and where are we going?" a wag has answered: North Americans are the only people in the history of the world to have gone from barbarism to decadence without passing through civilization.

Events surrounding the tragic Oklahoma bombing in 1995 suggest this is not far off the mark. They underline the irony of modernism, and have elicited feverish finger-pointing from media in the desperate search for a deep-culture scapegoat.

The irony lies in the fact that for the first time in world history, millions of human beings, the bulk of them North Americans, have the presumed advantages of plentiful food, high-tech toys, and rapid transportation. (Europeans here are still amazed to see the private cars of common labourers parked at job sites.) The assumption underlying this unqualified material and technological success has always been that once the masses were adequately comfortable, nations would be nice. Peaceful.

Instead, this century has been the bloodiest in history: Genocides. Gas chambers. Concentration camps. Rapine governments. Incomprehensible arsenals of nuclear destruction that squat, barely haltered, in any nation with a few bucks to rub together. No peace.

And we are discovering that it is this same high-tech world that enables not only evil nations, but evil individuals to deliver unerring and catastrophic death at the beep of a cellular phone, or the flick of a microwave detonator in the trunk of a medium-priced car.

If the British writer John Gray is correct that our continent resembles politically a "civil religion," then we can expect a lot more disruption. By this phrase he meant that for the first time in history the settlement of this vast virgin continent offered a whole people fleeing persecution, and armed with an absolutist theological worldview, the chance to create the New Jerusalem. Civilization was to begin anew, uncorrupted.

The settlers' most passionate concern was religious freedom. They wanted the freedom to bind themselves to their preferred religion and its moral code, creating their own moral communities without governments telling them what to believe. Deeply anti-government, many died for this right.

However, as secularism spread, moral bonds weakened, leaving the old hunger for freedom intact, minus the moral restraint — the "responsibility" that U.S. president Bill Clinton recently said "was coupled" (past tense) to freedom.

Fact is, the righteous secular elites simply decided that if there is to be no Heaven up there, why, we'll darn well make one down here, and almost any means are justified in building the New Jerusalem, the perfect egalitarian society. So more equality had to mean more government. Why not?

This switch spawned a reaction, the result being that now we have not one but two civil religions. The first (mostly modern leftists) has focused so much on redistributive rights to social benefits and equal outcomes that the whole ship is sinking. The second (mostly modern rightists) comprises millions of distraught individuals — not the silent, but the silenced, majority — plunking for freedom from big government and its legal plunder, for property rights, free enterprise, family, and religious rights. These different visions of the good society have formed a watershed of political foment from the beginning.

This distinction between modern leftists and rightists yields a further irony found in both American and Canadian history, in that the slogans of the modern, so-called "right-wing" militia groups now hunkering down in America echo almost exactly — but without the elegance — the sentiments of such as Thomas Paine, America's most famous eighteenth-century "left-winger." Liberty, this highly praised democratic populist wrote ringingly, is "wholly owing to the constitution of the people, and not to the constitution of the government." So it seems the root ideas haven't changed, but the labels have.

For when both our nations were cobbled together, it was the right-wingers of old — especially the Tory John A. Macdonald in Canada, and James Madison in America — who argued for strong central government. They were universally frightened of the "radicals" — the pro-democracy and therefore (by definition) "left-wingers" on both sides of the border who wanted minimal government, no taxes (at least certainly not without direct approval of the people), only direct democracy (no delegation, or representation), and strong state-provincial rights.

Such anti-government radicals saw themselves as defenders of the purest principles of democracy and the American Revolution, against all forms of foreign or national oppression, and cried out against betrayal of those principles by conservative statists who nevertheless, by a very narrow margin, did manage to impose their centralizing constitutional views on the states.

And so, quite weirdly, in America and Canada today it is the so-called "right wing" Republican Party and the Reform Party, respectively, that are shouldering the anti-government, low-tax mantle of direct popular democracy, against the liberal "left-wingers" who, through universal promotion of debt-financed welfarism and centralizing big government, have ruined their own New Jerusalem.

In other words, the new right has had to take over the philosophy and methods of the old left, because the new left has become too old right. Get it?

CAN DEMOCRACY BE MORAL?

WHEN THE NATIONAL media grabbed the headlines over the alleged physician-killing of Sue Rodriguez, Preston Manning and his Reform Party of Canada were thrown into a quandary that strikes right at the heart of popular democracy as a method of government.

On the divisive issue of euthanasia, Manning held several "electronic town hall" meetings to sound out the opinion of the people. Somewhat squeamishly, the party seems to hold that even if the will of the people runs dead against an MP's personal conscience, he or she must express that will. This is the basic stance of all popular democracy.

Such logic compels us to ask: So why not just pick a rep out of the phone book? For that matter, why pick anyone? Why don't the people just send a letter to a vote-counting parliamentary computer by overnight courier? The answer leads straight to a conflict between two irreconcilable views of truth under democracy.

For a leader, truth is permanent.

Politicians who consider themselves leaders, rather than delegates, will take the classical conservative view, as outlined from ancients such as Plato to moderns such as T. S. Eliot. As distinct from their finger-in-the-wind counterparts, such conservatives believe that the greatest moral truths of life are absolute, permanent, and unchanging. There are enduring values that must be discovered through reflection and experience, and relied upon by wise leaders. Once discovered, and only then, the proper political and moral judgements can be made, unaffected by how many might vote this way, or that, on Monday or Tuesday. Moral truth, in other words, like 2+2=4, cannot be altered by voting.

For a delegate, truth is a matter of popularity.

The delegate, however, unlike the leader, sees himself as empowered to express the will of the people, which he equates with what is desirable, with the good. Soon, pleasing the masses at every opportunity by removing all restraints on their will becomes the highest priority (and — not incidentally — the reaping of a corresponding popularity). Technical methods such as electronic town halls facilitate such direct expressions of mass desire.

The key to understanding the role of the modern secular-liberal delegate is his underlying assumption that there is no such thing as immutable truth — and probably should not be. For only if truth is relative can society be engineered towards perfection by way of continuously updated "progressive" policies. That is why, instead of weighing values, the liberal prefers to count them. Unfortunately, this essentially democratic process — equating the good with sheer numbers — is the dark side of democracy, for it opens the door to democratic tyrants.

That's why Eliot said in 1934 that "the forces of deterioration are a large crawling mass, and the forces of development are half a dozen men." This was just before a large crawling mass of utopian collectivists marched over a darkened, and soon bloodied, Europe. They had been directly and enthusiastically voted into power by well-educated, democratic majorities. Hitler fiercely defended his national socialism as "the truest democracy" (Berlin, Jan. 30, 1937), and described himself as an "arch-democrat."

What is the answer to this conflict at the heart of democracy, and why do we see those with conservative, absolute-truth instincts, such as Manning, promoting liberal, relative-truth techniques?

Perhaps the answer is that we live in a time when our elected representatives, rather than attending to remote national matters such as defence, fiscal policy, and foreign affairs, are intruding into the most intimate and detailed aspects of local, private, business, and family life, and plundering the energies of the people through taxation and debt to do so. Therefore, direct democracy — a kind of bottom-up revolution against a top-down political system — seems the only solution to rid us of such tyranny.

In most practical matters, such as taxation levels, this is likely a safe device. But when it comes to moral matters, such as euthanasia, abortion, capital punishment, homosexual incursions on the family, and so on, an elected representative has a duty first of all to make his conscience known before he is elected. After that, he should vote with his conscience — or resign. And for democracy itself, the notion that deeply moral choices ought to be shaped directly by the emotions of the moment — whether felt by one voter, or a million — is the route to self-destruction.

That is because as often as not, the correct moral choices both in life and politics require us (quite contrary to the dominant secular-liberal view) to choose not for but against our own appetites and desires in the interests of a higher good. But there can be no higher good in a relative world. That's why at such times political power ends up dictating every outcome. The democratic dilemma will not be resolved until our civilization decides once again to think through these two conflicting notions of how democracy is to be moral.

SUFFOCATED BY DO-GOODERS

THAT ELEGANT DEFENDER of the
free society, Charles Montesquieu (d.1755), to whom so much
is owed for the creation of modern liberties, knew better than
most how liberty ends. It inevitably falls victim to the craze
for an enforced political and social equality, or uniformity,
fuelled by ferocious envy and coercion. Sometimes, even a
great mind may fall victim to this folly, he warned, but "it
infallibly strikes small ones."

The recent United Nations Conference on Population and
Development was yet another globaloney love-in for 18,000
of these equalizers, who are now back home planning ways to
extract $17 billion (U.S.) from the rest of the world to fuel
their "cultural revolution."

They're culture-hip now, because economic socialism,

after wasting, oh, somewhere between 50 and 100 million human beings in the name of equality since 1917, through labour camps, forced famine, and liquidation, only equalized misery. Then it all crashed rather spectacularly on a Monday in January 1990. Poof!

So the economic radicals said, "It's not my fault," and overnight became social and sexual radicals. If you can't forcibly equalize people's incomes, why, then, go for their minds and values. The public may be excused for any looming sense of, well . . . let's call it suffocation by do-gooders.

So these legions of crushed believers are now the true dinosaurs of our time, and they're out there foraging with a vengeance. Annual U.N. "Summits" are just the collective grunting of this distraught and hungry herd when, about once every twelve months, they smell a new, and very green, food source, most often baled in U.S. denominations and guaranteed to supply them with more tenure and power.

Alas, the Deep Thinkers will never get it. They haven't figured out that the trade-off for civilization is not liberty *and* equality, but liberty *or* equality. They haven't figured out that more equality of this kind means more government, and absolute equality, absolute government.

Forging ahead, they have just informed the globe that "the family" is the basic unit of society. Yet the U.N.'s slogan for the family is "the smallest democracy at the heart of society." Now that's delirious. Laughable. Families democratic? Just try to imagine all the parents of the world asking their children to vote each morning on whether or not they ought to go to school, or use good manners, or respect their elders.

What's the U.N.'s motive? Simple. The family defined as a

democracy helps undermine parental authority and shifts power to children who, once armed with their new U.N.-defined "rights," will, as minors, then need to rely on lots of social workers and bureaucrats to assert these rights against their parents and society. Get it? It's a full-employment program in disguise.

Then we are told that the "empowerment" of women is crucial to the world; that men and women should "participate" in productive and reproductive life, and should "share responsibility" for children and housekeeping. Countries are ordered to "eliminate inequalities" between men and women as soon as possible.

Normally, humans "participate" in and "share" things voluntarily. But what this empowerment notion clearly implies is that women as a victim class are too stupid and docile to "empower" themselves, so a new status is to be conferred on them through enforced, tax-funded social and "reproductive rights" programs.

In the Deep Thinker sense, this means that all men and women shall think, value, feel, and work exactly the same way, as dictated and measured by Summit criteria. Sweden has already introduced programs to enforce this sort of automaton herd-behaviour through its government "Daddy Group." The Group actually withholds bonuses from all fathers who simply do not wish to spend their first three months at home on tax-funded paid leave with each newborn. Any free-minded person would surely judge a Swede an idiot for accepting such state regulation of personal life. But Swedes have no choice.

So finally from Cairo we get the most mindless feminist

slogan of all, "my body, my right." This is trotted out to justify state-financed mother-murder of babies if they are considered inconvenient in any way. They call it "health care." (With exceptions. Feminists say you mustn't abort the mildly disabled, or for sex-selection reasons, but if they're perfectly healthy — why, it's down the toilet!)

If you retort that women ought more often to exercise their moral right to refuse the risks of sex in the first place — or accept the human consequences — they will plead they had no choice. They could not help themselves. In other words, if I mess my doorstep, society cleans it up. But they are not "controlling" birth, as G. K. Chesterton observed. They are ensuring there isn't any birth to control. Let's get the language straight.

Add to that the U.N.'s exhortation for nations to sidestep parental authority and supply all "adolescents" with tax-funded "confidential" sex information and "education," and . . . what can I say? Such programs were meant to reduce sexually transmitted diseases, teen pregnancies, and abortions. Yet everywhere they have been introduced, all three have risen dramatically.

Everything considered, what we have here is yet another neat little anti-capitalist, anti-freedom, anti-family socialist revolution from the top, engineered by the world's liberal elites, and funded once again by the sucker taxpayers of the world. You and me, that is.

CRAZY PEOPLE DON'T REALLY LAUGH

THE IDEA THAT INDIVIDUALS may lose their way is easy to grasp. It happens all the time. And we know that a lot of loners go loopy because they lack the mirror of humanity in which to see themselves reflected.

Individuals get their reality therapy — sometimes shock therapy — from others who kindly or roughly scold them for being lost in some self-blinding "enthusiasm" (as our predecessors would have put it).

A recent example struck home. Tensions were building between a known feminist and . . . a male. And those of us watching the coming conflagration were getting very edgy. The male was asked for a character reference, so to speak, on another female. "She's a bitch," he said, knowing this would send up the feminist. True to form, she pierced him mercilessly with red-hot poker eyes, then shot back with her best rhetorical weaponry: "That's terrible! What would you call her if she were a man?"

We held our breath for the fireworks. And without missing a beat, and perhaps somewhat alarmed, he blurted out — "a son of a bitch."

Well, there was a spontaneous and delightful burst of laughter —real, hearty belly laughter — from everyone present, and the laughter most enjoyable and enjoyed was from the feminist and the male, who were now bending over in stitches, momentarily beautiful and happy because freed by spontaneous humour from a narrow frame of mind. Our whole society needs a shot of that.

But humour is only possible if we are still sane. Crazy people don't really laugh, for they have lost the corrective tension between the true and the absurd. For them, everything is absurd.

Neither do whole nations laugh. And the fear is surely that whole nations, just like individuals, can sink into absurdity . . . and think it normal.

Some recent events that come to mind are like little markers along the way: the "correctness" scandal at the University of British Columbia in 1995, in which an "outraged" woman spent a quarter-million tax dollars to report that some professors have bad manners; and stories about the need for "volunteer community mediators" to solve disputes in schools and neighbourhoods. Both cause reflection on a saying we will surely have increasing cause to ponder. Namely, that in a free society, "there can be no public good without private virtue."

If private virtue is anything, it must be a proper sense of balance, or discernment, which is an inner thing having to do with self-control — with balancing the spiritual, rational, and physical parts of our being. And if wildly expensive and silly correctness reports and yellow-shirted police-students in schoolyards indicate anything, it is a serious loss of this inner control. "The parents and teachers have failed," was one observation, "because adults without control and manners are just young people who never learned them."

Unfortunately, people who lose the ability to correct themselves soon lose the confidence to correct others, such as their children, their students, or other bad-mannered adults. Then we have to ask some legal agency, or volunteer mediator, to do the job. In essence, we take each other to behaviour court.

Modern liberal society is vainly attempting to externalize controls that we should insist remain internal, by slipping the powers of surveillance and behaviour modification to external agents. Such desperate bureaucratic measures to enforce a frivolous notion of the public good are signs we have given up on private virtue.

The real danger, of course, is that we have brought this distinctly unhumorous regime upon ourselves as a consequence of deliberate political theory. For in the egalitarian kingdom of modern liberalism it is not nice to be good, or speak of goodness. For this implies someone else may not be good. That's why a regime of radical equality, as one insightful critic put it, will always produce "a legal disestablishment of morality" by getting rid of any good, better, best, standard of behaviour. Not tolerance, but neutrality, then becomes the standard, lest some be hurt, or stigmatized.

This all seems part of a shift from the old notion of self-improvement (which required some genuine standard against which to judge ourselves and others), to the modern, self-flattering notion of self-esteem (which is a silly notion, simply because esteem is something granted by others according to our actions, not according to our own opinion of ourselves). It's also a shift from the idea of divine providence, to political providence (and thus, to more taxes).

To complete this politically providential circle, we call for more and better policies, pleasing ourselves with an illusion of the public good in compensation for weakened private virtue. This in turn requires abandoning and neutralizing the major moral issues, long since consigned to arbitration by the state and its charters (lest we offend whole groups in society), and venting our residual moral outrage on the little things that are left. Sound familiar?

THE MOST EVIL
LIE OF ALL?

Some say the sign of a decent civilization is how we treat the poor. But a better guide is how well we protect women and children from sexual predators.

Faced with a bevy of homophilic judgements from courts and tribunals, critics in a mood of resigned premonition have warned that there are now no viable grounds to stop the normalization, protection, and promotion of pedophilia. Canada's gay Member of Parliament, Svend Robinson, has complained bitterly when the homosexual-pedophilia connection is made, saying it "is the most hateful . . . most evil lie of all." But is it?

At the 1994 International Gay and Lesbian Association conference, many delegates protested as bitterly against throwing out NAMBLA, the North American Man-Boy Love Association, shouting: "Pedophilia is about love, not child abuse."

Alas, the homosexual and pedophilia wagons have both been hitched to the rogue horse of modern liberalism: all sexual expression is good because unrestrained human freedom is good. Toronto's Gerald Hannon, a homosexual prostitute and professor at Ryerson Polytechnic University whose lengthy defences of homo-erotic life are often printed in the *Globe and Mail*, and who describes himself as a man with "a healthy commitment to depravity," writes that homosexual liberation is "about the liberation of all people." He recalls, approvingly, "watching some pornography in which two ten-year-old boys fucked each other."

Needless to say, most homosexuals are not pedophiles, and repudiate it in principle. But radical homosexuals, sexologists, and philosophers are another matter. By mid-century, Alfred Kinsey, author of the influential Kinsey Report, was having one-year-old babies masturbated by workers in his sex "laboratories" in an effort to prove they are capable of sexual arousal. He advocated child sex with adults as a healthy part of growing up. His co-worker, Wardell Pomeroy, actively defends "intergenerational sex" in the courts.

The newer generation of anti-authority homosexual liberals is even more militant and has latterly discovered the tired "deconstruction" movement that drifted our way from Jacques Derrida and Michel Foucault of France twenty years ago. They say the idea that there is some moral norm supporting social behaviour is merely a cover for elite power. All forms of social authority (taboos, restrictions, morals, laws) are just "constructed" by power-holders for their benefit as a class. So down with them, is the solution. And up with liberation.

This mood has been linked in the liberal (and especially in the homosexual) mind with the notion of "consent" as a validation of any freely chosen behaviour, whether abortion, euthanasia — or pedophilia. The 1972 U.S. National Gay Rights platform calls for the abolition of all laws governing age of consent. Child sex is not wrong, they argue, if the target child agrees. (You can see the brown bag full of candy coming out of the raincoat pocket.) NAMBLA says, "People [meaning young boys] should be free to affirm their own values." The October 1991 issue of this organization's *Bulletin* gave a New York 1-800 number to send for lists of children needing adoption.

The obvious error is that a child may consent to eating only popcorn every day, to trying Russian roulette, or watching porn movies. But this is agreement, not consent. The latter has always implied a standard of maturity — a knowledge of self and consequences — more reliable than mere appetite or fascination. Age-of-consent laws protect children from predatory males with beguiling arguments.

Now it is true that heterosexuals commit most child sex abuse. But that's because at least 96 percent of the population is heterosexual. Homosexuals are only about 1 to 2 percent of the population (with occasional bisexuals included, it may come to 4 percent). But because homosexuality has now been legally normalized, and activist pedophiles hang their main argument on seeking a meaningless consent from children, what we need to answer is the question, "Do homosexuals indeed figure disproportionately in the sexual molestation of children?"

It doesn't look good. A 1985 survey in the *Los Angeles*

Times showed that homosexuals perpetrate between one-third and one-half of all child molestations. Good studies show that proportional rates for homosexual molestation of pupils by teachers is especially high — up to 80 percent of all cases. A 1991 British Columbia Ministry of Health study reviewed 2,099 cases of child sexual abuse, and found that 94 percent of perpetrators were male — and 50 percent of victims were boys, mostly under twelve. The Canadian Centre for Justice Statistics, studying the decade 1980–89, found the same. Perpetrators, 91 percent male. Victims, 46.5 percent young boys. Go figure.

So the facts are not in question and, regrettably, neither are the politics. For sure, the next campaign in the name of democratic freedom and equality rights will be the legalization of pedophilia in a "pedophobic" society. The bible of psychiatry, the *Diagnostic and Statistical Manual*, has already watered down the definition of pedophilia to suggest that a man who molests children is only a pedophile if he feels badly about it. Another harbinger is that the age of consent for homosexual sodomy — recently reduced by courts to fourteen in Canada — has already been lowered to twelve in Holland . . . as long as the parents of the child agree. It's no wonder liberalism has become a dirty word.

MORAL VISION, MORAL SOCIETY

JUSTICE MINISTER Allan Rock
has spoken for the state, to the effect that if the people
cannot accept his "gay-rights" measures, then to hell with
them. But if the people were to speak for themselves, what
might they say? Perhaps something like this:

We are not intolerant. In fact, we are prepared to suspend our
public, but not our private, moral judgement for a sometimes
alarming range of behaviours. Neither are we "homophobic,"
which is a silly term. We are not afraid of homosexuals. We
are mostly disgusted by homosexual behaviour and the
homosexual worldview.

We think the claim that homosexuals only want equal
"civil rights" is offensive, because homosexuals cannot be
distinguished from other human beings except by their

behaviour, which is changeable, as is all behaviour.

No one knows what "causes" homosexuality, any more than they know what causes, say, alcoholism, or drug abuse, but we do not attempt to promote or normalize either of these. And the fact is that credible psychiatrists and sexologists claim cure rates of about 70 percent. University of Toronto psychiatry professor Joseph Berger has said, "I have never come across anyone with 'innate homosexuality.' That notion [is a] gay-activist political position . . . It has zero scientific foundation."

At any rate, we cannot wait upon "research" to tell us what is morally or socially good. Wise leaders know that only moral vision creates a moral society, and that ultimately we all must answer the question: What model shall we uphold for our young as the preferred social arrangement for the rearing and protection of future generations?

Clearly, this must be a procreational model that specifically favours the married mother and father and their dependent children. Others may choose, or even be forced by circumstances, to live in other ways. But this does not imply an obligation on society to favour or promote those ways as equally desirable objectives for society as a whole. After all, the mere idea of a society that encourages its young men to roam about attempting to convert the male anus into a vagina is plainly insane.

As a free people, of course, we must argue that individuals have rights. But surely a society — which is not simply a collection of individuals but has a being, a nature of its own — has higher rights, among them its ancient right to design and promote intentionally preferential policies and tax codes to protect its preferred model of social behaviour. To encourage good love, that is.

Homosexuals often claim they "love" their partners, therefore they have a claim to the same social privileges and benefits as heterosexual couples. But all societies distinguish between good and bad love. Self-love, or narcissism, is notoriously bad love. Sexual love of children (pedophilia) is bad love. Incest is universally declared bad love. So is sado-masochism, polygamy, necrophilia, bestiality, and so on. There are thousands of forms of bad love.

In contrast to these, our Judeo-Christian tradition teaches that good love ranges in quality and purity from its most basic forms, such as innocent affection for the animals and plants of the earth, upwards to love of close friends, neighbours, and family, to love of our own children, to love of our spouse, to spiritual love of God. The mere claim to a feeling of "love," in other words, is not automatically a sanction for the behaviour it is used to justify.

We believe the heart of civil society is the sexual order with its four classic, interconnected prohibitions relating to number, gender, age, and incest. The number prohibition states that you can only marry one person at a time; gender, that you can only marry someone of the opposite sex; age, that you cannot marry someone below a certain age; and incest, that you cannot have sex with immediate blood relations. These protect society against polygamy, homosexuality, pedophilia, and genetic disorder.

We are aware that the homosexual movement is only a part of a much broader, pansexual movement dedicated to the destruction of this sexual order. Pansexualism argues that because we are all naturally good, then all consenting sex must be good. Pansexualists say that guilt, shame, taboos, and prohibitions against polygamy, homosexuality, pedophilia, and incest (the sexual order) are products of a "sex-negative" society and must be eliminated by an aggressive attack on "hetero-normativity."

What pansexualists really want is to replace our Judeo-Christian sexual order, one based on self-restraint and procreation, with a new, merely sensual order, based on self-indulgence and recreation. They are sexual radicals and their tactics are piecemeal. If they can persuade us to agree that gender doesn't matter, then soon the number of spouses, their age, or their blood relationship to us won't matter, either. Sexologist Alfred Kinsey's partner Wardell Pomeroy, for example, has argued that sex with animals is fine, as long as you don't hurt the animal. Like Kinsey, he promotes "consensual," or "positive" incest, both for pleasure and as a social bulwark against the spread of AIDS, STDs, and promiscuity. In other words, if young Johnny gets the urge, he should just whistle for the family dog, or jump in bed with his young sister, or maybe even his mother.

They are welcome to their vision. But it should not be affirmed, protected, or promoted.

VIII

Some Matters of Conviction

*The only thing necessary
for the triumph of evil
is for good men to do nothing.*

— EDMUND BURKE, 1770

HE KNEW WHAT
HE STOOD FOR

A GOOD FRIEND ONCE SAID that even in the face of the most depressing situations, we have a duty to be optimists. Life's an attitude thing. It becomes what you make of it. His defining example was the two little boys who, when led into a playroom, saw only a miserable pile of manure in the corner. The first little boy burst into tears because he didn't see any toys. The second burst into leaps of joy, and ran around the room shouting, "With all this manure, there's got to be a pony somewhere!"

All right, so most of the time, it works. Any situation can be turned to the better. At the extreme, though, mere optimism is a bore. It becomes a determined cheerfulness. The kind of fatalism we see in the person who is happy he got a flat tire and missed his appointment, because otherwise he might have continued on and been killed in an accident.

Most annoying of all, perhaps, is the sort of person who refers to every problem as "a challenge." There's something eerily unreal about these people: smiling, pure-bred positive thinkers who strike us as never really having thought at all. For them, nothing is ever deeply wrong. Cosmically wrong. Or cosmically right. It's just temporarily out of order, and needs to be fixed.

That's why rarely these days do we ever see a true fit of pique or sustained bloody outrage. I don't mean those too frequent and ridiculous shows of indignant emotion seen everywhere for the sake of some injured personal feeling, or on account of some perceived sexual or racial slight pawned off as an offence against humanity.

I mean the kind of booming, articulate, forceful, scolding display trotted out in colourful language that sets things straight, and no fooling around. You know, the kind that used to flow from supremely self-confident people — a legendary grandparent, perhaps, or the sort of teacher who marked you indelibly for life.

The headmaster of our school, the Reverend J. A. M. "Rusty" Bell, was that way. We could see it coming from a long way off. He would stride purposively towards the assembly hall in his flowing academic black gown, his head tilted forward, cheeks already somewhat reddened by the urgent preoccupations of his mind. A kind of pre-emptive wariness would flow over the mob of students, and a great wonderment, too. Somewhere, deep in the soul, each of us silently braced ourselves for the spectacle to come.

And come, it did. After our noisy lunch. As if merely from

the rustle of his robes, the very moment Rusty Bell stood up, a great silence fell upon the room like a stone. In that brief moment between his standing and his first words — not loud, necessarily, but always, *always*, having that boom of reasoned moral authority — the minds of all three hundred students and our teachers seemed to snap to attention. In his impressive way he was about to take some event of misconduct by a student (or perhaps by the whole school) that we had hardly noticed, and in the burning adjectives and searing imagery that flew from under his thick red shocks of hair, and flashed from his genuinely pained eyes, persuade us, without a doubt, of our wrongdoing.

Afterwards, there was always a general sense that things would be all right for a while, because he had straightened them, and us, out. For here was a man who knew what he thought, and why he thought it, and said so unerringly and impressively. He was a grounded man, rich in bias and prejudice, not in the narrow modern sense that he sought to offend, but in the traditional sense that he knew what he stood for. A man, he felt, ought to be biased in favour of what is good, and against what is bad. And a man without prejudice, in the sense of knowing what he thinks about things most serious, and able vigorously to defend them, is rudderless, without thoughts at all. A weakling.

And he knew, too, in contrast to the modern gospel, that a man's personal preferences, or "rights," were utterly secondary to the lifelong job of grasping the truth. In other words, and paradoxically, he gave the sense of being planted deeply in the soil of a rich personal life, precisely because he made personal preferences secondary. Rumour has it that a few days before the end of his life, he read an extended and fiery riot act to a stunned hospital staff on the miseries of technology and modern dying, disentangled himself from wires and tubes, and dragged himself home to expire in his own bed.

Alas, those days are over. As the Bard put it, ours is a weak, piping time of peace, in which we worry most about offending because we cannot agree on what is truly offensive. Therefore anything may be. Our deepest fear is that someone will dislike us for our convictions, so we arrange to have none. Publicly.

Of course, most people still have wonderful private fits, mostly in their minds, long after the event that provoked them. Often it's in the form of an imaginary debate while driving alone to work. Our absent opponent withers before an onslaught of exquisite, highly persuasive argument we didn't quite manage in reality.

You can see such people, their mouths motoring away behind the window of many a passing car. Sometimes their heads actually nod in self-agreement. Sometimes they will even take both hands off the wheel at once and wave them in the air to make a point. Sometimes they suddenly look at you, and you know you've been caught at the same thing.

SMALL DEATH, BIG LESSON

T HERE WAS A BIG LESSON in a small death at the farm this week. Some say death is a friend. But I still have trouble getting used to that idea. Seems like a con job floated by the really fearful. In my youth, the defiant poet Dylan Thomas spoke to us richly when he wrote, "Do not go gently into that good night/ Old age should burn and rave at close of day/ Rage, rage, against the dying of the light." Yessir. Death was the enemy. The lesson was that by their mere presence, children rescue adult experience from hardness and banality and force unanticipated self-reflection.

Here I was in the barn, quietly forking manure into the wheelbarrow, when I saw the frightened eyes of a cute baby pigeon staring at me from the shadows along the wall. For a week, five times a day, I shoved an eyedropper of food down its gullet. Flying lessons twice daily. But infallibly it was back on the ground, with no brakes. Or stuck in a pine tree, upside down. Aw, let it go.

No, let's keep feeding it, was the general resolve. We'll take it to the cottage, Dad. Can we? Oh please? My fourteen-year-old daughter was already in love ("It" was now "Tweedy"). In a few hours she got Tweedy to perch on the edge of the box and fly almost five feet, on a bit of a downslope, to her out-stretched hand whenever she called. This farm life is great, I thought. Lots of opportunity for love and bonding. At Christmas, our baby goat was born. Yesterday, a huge, hand-some coyote was just yards from our pond. (Though a month ago a pack of them tore apart a neighbour's dog, and we got nature's double message.)

Then it happened. I confess now, in some pain, the bread pellets were my idea. Tweedy feasted on them, pecking happily, as my daughter laid them before her. But within an hour, she was labouring for breath. Heart racing. Three kids shouted for me in unison panic.

Here we were, at the lake, on an island, an hour from the nearest town on a Sunday, in a rainstorm. My daughter begged, "Call the ambulance, Dad. She's sick." A lovely, if impractical request. But there was no time for talk about hierarchies of living things. Tweedy was falling over a lot, and there was no chance for the Heimlich manoeuvre on a pigeon. This was a tight spot. Three pairs of terror-stricken eyes on a helpless hero Dad failing badly. Panic mounted steeply. "Dad! Do something. Please!"

"I'm trying! I'm trying!" It was horrible to watch. So, hoping to relieve their anxiety and teach lower animal mercy, I said

if she's in pain for too long, we'll have to end it. What a boo-
boo that was. "Daaaaaad! you mean . . . kill Tweedy? How
could you?" From mercy to cruelty in one glance. There
would be a long death-watch. But suddenly Tweedy fell forward
on her own neck. Then, in some sharp foreknowledge of the
good night to come, her frantic wings propelled her in a wild
death spin right before our widened eyes, 'til she toppled one
last time, folded in silence.

All choked up, I couldn't actually say, "She's dead," to their
faces. Instead, I took her frail body in my hands, and said,
"Her heart has stopped." My tearful daughter blamed herself
for feeding Tweedy the bread. It wasn't the bread, I said. She
was sick. For sure, she had some illness. It was . . . natural.

Bad word choice. "Natural, Dad"? How can something so
horrible and sad, be "natural"? It was a question about justice.
My two young sons stared quietly ahead: "We've never seen
something actually . . . die . . . before." They buried Tweedy,
deep, with mournful, intense respect, in a cereal box, a rock
and a flower on top. A universal rite of passage, their first
funeral.

Once back home, the memory of sweet Tweedy faded. But
routine experience was once again transformed when my
youngest son followed me on a trip to the barn to see if I had
trapped one of the three rats feeding on our grain. Then out of
the blue came the unexpected question: "Can we keep them,
Dad? I got a cage." On the spot again.

No. The farmer next door says: "You got a rat? Well, there's a
nine-times rule. If you seen one, you got nine. There's
twenty-seven rats somewhere in that barn." Soon there'll be
a hundred. Tweedy was cute. Rats are disgusting. I hear him

say, "No they're not," just as I see that the trap isn't there.

It's three feet away, halfway down a dark hole. For sure, my boy now has a fast-freeze image of a cute, badly squeezed little fellow backing down the hole. There was a bath of relief as I gingerly pulled out what felt like a free trap ("he escaped!"), when horror struck again. We both saw a little arm with its curled pink fist pinched tightly in the trap — gnawed off at the elbow.

Now, without my son present, there would have been a flicker of mature disgust, and into the garbage with it. Instead, here I was, reluctantly holding this gruesome trophy, lost for words. Rodent banality was transformed into a welter of questions about the life force; about how even the lowliest creature could sacrifice its own arm in a rage against the dying of the light. Children do soften us all. I know my son felt God was a witness to this heinous act, and just in case there was any doubt, he let me know he was on God's side. So there was no point mentioning the poison that would now be needed. I couldn't face any more attitude adjustment.

FROM "A HISSING CAULDRON OF LUST" TO THE MIND OF GOD

CHRISTMAS DAY

WHAT ARE WE TO THINK of a man who tells God, "I defied you, even so far as to relish the thought of lust, and to gratify it, too — within the walls of your church, during the celebration of your mysteries."

He was a daring, in-your-face iconoclast. A wild fornicator, with many mistresses and a bastard son. A self-confessed thief who declared "the evil in me was foul, but I loved it." How's that for modern liberation?

Those words were written in A.D. 398 by Saint Augustine, one of the fullest sinners and greatest saints in all of Christendom, in his *Confessions*, a book appropriate for reading during Christmas week.

So the thought came to me that the power and the beauty of Augustine's physical and spiritual struggles, all sparked by

Christ's birthday, are still, in microcosm, the ongoing and unsettled struggles of our anti-spiritual time.

Everywhere in the churches of this secular land we see sparse congregations, grey hair, and lots of women. Our spiritually hungry youth, seeking fire, discover there mostly boredom and ashes. And yet the greatest surprise in reading Augustine is not preachiness, not scolding analysis — but fire. His overwhelming passion. His burning emotional, sensual, and intellectual fervour.

His struggles centred on three main problems: the flesh, good and evil, and the cosmos.

As a youth, he travelled to Carthage to study, where, he writes, "I found myself in the midst of a hissing cauldron of lust." Sounds like a modern university.

There, he says he twisted in the chains of pleasure, and loved it, "wallowing in filth and scratching the itching sore of lust." But he soon felt submerged by pleasure, locked in a mortal struggle with his own appetites, beyond which he saw nothing. So one day he cried out half-heartedly for relief, begging God, "give me chastity and continence — but not yet." He was still a young deal-maker.

And where are we today but drowning in sensuality, submerged in it as a people. We live in a time when mainstream newspapers cannot be left open for young eyes, so filled are they with embarrassingly raw discussions and depictions of sex, and near adoration of what Augustine called the "sin of Sodom." He struggled against this sensual suffocation, in search of a higher truth.

His resolution was to argue that if there was a God, then He himself must be the highest, most perfect love, downward from which other forms of love flowed, to the basest love of our most beastly and binding appetites. Therefore it is imperative for us not only to distinguish among and rank the forms of love, but actively to repudiate the worst and seek the best. To discriminate.

In so freeing himself from the fetters of mere passion, Augustine strongly shaped the moral hierarchies of the Western world — and thereby freed it to pursue the same heights. It is a world now busily repudiating his lesson in the name of egalitarian pluralism and diversity, a world that says there is nothing higher, and everything is equally good.

So back into the chains we go.

Having solved the question "What is good?" Augustine then agonized over how it is possible to have a good God and a bad world. For ten years he argued — mistakenly, he came to say — that both good and evil were substances, like things, and just as his own spirit struggled with his flesh, the good and evil God put on earth are locked in the struggle.

He freed himself from this idea by reasoning that if God was good, his whole cosmos must be good. Therefore evil could not come from these good things, but from a misuse of the will. Evil was an idea. This conclusion, too, has shaped our moral life and our whole body of law, because it conceives of humans as moral agents capable of good or evil by choice. This is now a corrupted legacy in our society, the schools and courts of which are more likely to teach us that all bad behaviour is a result of low income, or socialization, or abuse of some kind; that crime is not our fault, but the fault of our environment.

We are back to the notion that evil springs from things.

Augustine's last struggle in the *Confessions*, like that of any youth straining to understand the stars, was with the existence of the cosmos itself. He undertakes an acute analysis of the nature of time, as a response to the ancient question, If God made the universe, what existed before the Big Bang?

His answer is that time is simply a function of moving physical things, such as planets and people. In itself, it does not exist, because the future is only what is not yet, and the past is only what has been, but is no longer. Behind things in time, there is only the ongoing present. Eternity. Just what was here when the universe in time was created.

Our way of undertaking the same interrogation is to send the $5 billion Hubble telescope into space to peer into the infinite, only to hear Stephen Hawking, the most fashionable cosmologist of our secular time, conclude on behalf of that most secular science of physics, that to know the answers to these questions will be "to know the mind of God."

Merry Christmas.